Women in the 21st Century Church

Written by Mary Louise Henning

Blessing Publication

Women in the 21st Century Church

Copyright 2015 Mary Louise Henning

Cover by Najla Qamber Designs

Blessing Publication ™

All rights reserved. No part of this publication may be reproduced, stored in a retrieval system, or transmitted in any form, or by any means—electronic, mechanical, photocopying, recording, or otherwise—except for brief quotations in printed reviews, without the prior written permission of the copyright owner.

~For my Mama, who continues to inspire and encourage me to achieve the impossible.~

Contents

Acknowledgments

Foreword

Introduction

Chapter 1	page 16
Chapter 2	page 38
Chapter 3	page 59
Chapter 4	page 75
Chapter 5	page 94
Chapter 6	page 112
Chapter 7	page 130
Chapter 8	page 146
Chapter 9	page 161
Chapter 10	page 171
Chapter 11	page 181
Chapter 12	page 192
Chapter 13	page 207
Conclusion	page 218
References	page 228

Acknowledgements

I am eternally grateful to so many who have poured into my sixty years of life. I am who I am because of your investment. My husband and best friend, Daryl, has supported, encouraged and believed that I could reach for the stars and attain my dreams. My sons, Jason and David, continually remind me that love has no limits. My daughter-in-law, Julie, has exceeded every expectation, and I am blessed to call my own. My grandchildren, Sarah Beth, Brittany, Rylan, and Sydney inspire me to leave a legacy of faith, hope and love in Christ Jesus, who can do all things. My sister, Lea, and my brother, Bill, have taught me that siblings are priceless, and your pride in me measures true achievement. My brother, Steve, has taught me that forgiveness is not conditional. My four step-children, twelve step grandchildren and nine step great-grandchildren have redefined "blended-family," for which I am most thankful. Mike Piburn, my advisor and friend, cheered me through Bible College and continues to encourage me to greater things. My publisher, Blessing Publication, took a chance on me and motivated me to race through the doors God opens. My dear friend, Phyllis Shaw, discipled me thirty years ago, and taught me to become a woman after God's own heart. That is where my journey began. I am continually humbled and blessed by God's amazing grace.

"This book, the accumulation of almost three and one-half years of study by Mary Louise grew out of her Senior Project for graduation. As I read through her manuscript, I decided, rather than mark it up for critique, to preserve it for my wife, daughters, and granddaughters to read. It became apparent to me that it deserved publication. Every woman should read this book to gain a clearer understanding of the call of God on her life. The church will benefit from women working through this book for personal enrichment or as a group study. It is that good."

Mike Piburn,
Director of Non-Traditional Studies
Calvary Bible College & Theological Seminary
Kansas City, Missouri

"In Women in the 21st Century Church, Mary Louise Henning has thoroughly done her homework. She writes historically with examples of the place of women in the Old and New Testaments. She writes contemporarily of the confusion of competing voices regarding the proper role of women, which has brought about discontentment and contributed to the deterioration of the family as well as impacted the church and society. She writes practically challenging the reader on how to have the most significant and blessed life possible. I commend this book to any woman, layman, or church leader who desires a clearer understanding of the place of women in the home, church, and world."

Wayne Robertson
Pastor, Morningside Baptist Church
Valdosta, Georgia

"If a woman wants to know how the God who created her wants her to live, then this is a book she will want to read. Mary Louise chooses women from both the Old and New Testaments and shows how God worked in their lives and then applies those principles to the twenty-first century woman. It is easy to read, and the truths of God's Word jump off the pages and into the mind and heart of the reader. Those truths can literally change a life."

Dr. Randall Terrill
Retired Pastor
Bartlesville, Oklahoma

Foreword

The premise of this excellent book is stated by the author, Mary Louise Henning, as "A woman's highest calling and deepest need is to know God." Mrs. Henning touches each area of today's woman from the perspective of a Bible character and biblical principles that are the basis of this book. The world's assertions that promote an egocentric view of the place and practice of women are addressed with a Bible-centered Christian worldview. This author presents clear explanation and goals for the person, the home, the church, the circles of friendship and the community enhancement of women in the twenty-first century. Any woman seeking to live a godly example in a world that has adopted pagan philosophies will profit greatly from this book.

Dr. Elwood H. Chipchase, President Emeritus
Calvary Bible College & Theological Seminary
Belton, Missouri

Introduction

On the surface, the Bible seems sexist, male dominated. The early church, governed and led by men, continues to be God's model for his church. Failure to read, study, and research God's Word accurately, to interpret it correctly, and to apply it truthfully leads to misunderstanding and misconception. Both the Old Testament and the New Testament give accounts of women who were primary participants in God's plan of redemption for mankind. It is through careful and prayerful reading, studying, researching and applying God's Word that we gain accurate knowledge and understanding of God's message to us. God created woman with a purpose and a plan and through her, Salvation entered the world. The message is clear: women are God's extraordinary, unique handiwork. From the beginning, "God saw all that he had made and it was very good." Nothing in Scripture indicates anything to the contrary.

Twenty one centuries of immeasurable societal evolution, cultural progress, and extreme change for women must be reconciled to the Bible. While that seems practically impossible from a worldview perspective, the Bible's simple message remains timeless. External change occurs at nanosecond speed. Yet woman, created in the image of God, for the purpose of God, has not changed. Twenty one centuries later, women continue to struggle to find purpose and value. That desperately sought after purpose and worth can only be found in Christ. In Him, we find our sustenance, our solace, and our divine purpose.

"I make known the end from the beginning, from ancient times what is still to come. My purpose will stand, and I will do all that I please." (Isaiah 46:10) NIV

Chapter 1

The First Lady

"So the Lord God caused a deep sleep to fall upon man, and he slept; then He took one of his ribs, and closed up the flesh at that place. And the Lord God fashioned into a woman the rib which He had taken from the man, and brought her to the man" (ESV Genesis 2:21-22). "The man called his wife's name Eve, because she was the mother of all living" (Genesis 3:20).

One of the first things that come to mind when we think of Eve is the role she played in the fall. After all, our nemesis is sin, and we have Eve, in part, to thank for its birth. Sin is a primary part of Eve's legacy, but there is a great deal more to Eve's biography than sin. The first lie originated in the Garden of Eden. It was the woman who fell for it, hook, line and sinker. The consequences of her action changed everything. That first sin completely distorted the roles of men and women and has led to the breakdown of the family, the church, and society as a whole.

The bombardment of lies from the Enemy has removed our focus from the Creator to one of self, whether in pride or failure. Centuries later, women are still struggling with the same issues Eve struggled with. Everything around us has changed beyond the imagination, yet we are still the same. We are the daughters of Eve. What does that signify for us? The task is to detangle the web of lies, establish facts, find the truth, and determine who we are in Christ. Who was Eve? "Eve wasn't formed from the dust of the earth like Adam, but carefully designed from living flesh and bone and the only being ever directly created by God from the living tissue of another creature" (MacArthur 2005, 1). This describes woman as unique in beauty, character, and significance. It is vital that women stop listening to the white noise of the world that bombards us with unrealistic expectations and seek truth for ourselves. We need to establish our origin. "Eve was created to know and walk with God and to make Him known to others by reflecting his character in her life. This is a woman's true path to fulfillment and meaning - the only way we will ever discover who we are and find our purpose" (Custis James 2005, 35).

Creation of Woman

"So God created man in His own image, in the image of God He created him, male and female He created them" (Genesis 1:27). Webster's Dictionary defines image as a physical likeness or representation of a person, animal, or thing, photographed, painted, sculptured, or otherwise made visible, form, appearance, semblance, counterpart, copy (Webster 2001, 404). Image in the Hebrew Old Testament means illusion, resemblance, a representative figure (NASB 1977, 99). "The creation of male and female shows God's image in (1) harmonious interpersonal relationships, (2) equality in personhood and importance, and (3) difference in role and authority" (Grudem 1999, 199). Women and men are created equally in God's image. We are of equal value and importance to Him. Neither man nor woman is the lesser. Eve was created in the image of God. "This is the starting point for any definition of what it means to be a woman" (Custis James 2005, 32).

The woman was created for the man, to help him, to support him, to come alongside him, to complement him, to complete him. These two creatures were unique in their humanity. They were created with intellect, emotion, ability, sensuality, and the ability to reason and to love. When Adam awoke after his surgery, from his deep sleep, he saw the woman and immediately fell in love with her. She was everything he never knew he needed – best friend, companion, helper, lover, soul mate. Creation took on a new meaning. Nothing else in creation compared to this woman. It was in this relationship that God instituted the marriage relationship, clearly between a man and a woman.

"Therefore a man shall leave his father and mother and hold fast to his wife, and they shall become one flesh" (Genesis 2:24). God designed man and woman physically to become one flesh, not only sexually, but emotionally, and in dependence on one another for completing the task assigned to them. "And God said to them, 'Be fruitful and multiply, and fill the earth and subdue it and have dominion over the fish of the sea, the birds of the heavens, and over every living thing that moves on the earth'" (Genesis 1:28). God ingrained marriage, family and children in the hearts of women. He gave her the desire to nurture, care for and mother his creation. No one can deny that women are exclusively the vessel through which human life evolves. There is nothing more profound, powerful or beautiful than creating and birthing a living, breathing human being.

Jesus, himself, took the form of humanity and entered the world through the birth canal of a woman. There is no greater evidence of the value of women.

Headship

Then God said, "Let us make man in our image, after our likeness" (Genesis 1:26a). The pronouns "us" and "our" are plurals, identifying God the Father, God the Son, and God the Holy Spirit as individual entities in one being. Image and likeness are interchangeable terms indicating that man was created in a natural and moral likeness of God. To understand the relationship of men and women and their roles, we must first understand the relationship of the Trinity. "Between the Trinity has been equality in importance, personhood and deity throughout all eternity. Each member of the Trinity has distinct roles and functions" (Grudem 1999, 202). God the Father, God the Son, and God the Holy Spirit are one, yet each has his own unique role and function. "God the Father has always been the Father and has always related to the Son as a Father relates to his Son. Though all three members of the Trinity are equal in power and in all attributes, the Father has greater authority. In creation, the Father speaks and initiates, but the work of creation is carried out through the Son and sustained by the continuing presence of the Holy Spirit" (Grudem 1994, 459). Man and woman have distinct roles and functions in the male/female relationship. With the understanding that the male/female relationship was designed in the image of the Trinity, we can better understand authority and headship. Then the Lord God said, "It is not good that man should be alone; I will make a helper fit for him" (Genesis 2:18).

Man and woman were created as equals, yet with separate roles, each to support and complement the other, to be subject to one another. These separate roles are equally important, equally necessary, and equally vital. Adam was created first. Eve was created from and for

Adam. In that order, God instituted headship and Adam was assigned the role. With it came an enormous responsibility for man. He alone is responsible to God for the welfare of his wife, children, and home. Man did not ask for the leadership role. It was mandated by God, and God holds man responsible and accountable in his role as leader. Consider the enormity of that command. Consider for a moment that God did woman a colossal favor in this arrangement.

Sin

In the Twenty-First Century, headship is viewed as chauvinistic, demeaning, and prejudiced. This erroneous thinking is a direct result of original sin. "The Lord God took the man and put him in the Garden of Eden to work it and keep it. And the Lord God commanded the man, saying, 'You may surely eat of every tree of the garden, but of the tree of the knowledge of good and evil you shall not eat, for in the day that you eat of it you shall surely die'"

(Genesis 2:15-17). Adam and Eve lived in a perfect world. Yet, it wasn't enough. We, too want more, different, better, happier circumstances.

In the Garden of Eden, Eve was deceived by the serpent and ate of the forbidden fruit of the tree of knowledge of good and evil. She gave the fruit to Adam, who willfully took it and ate. God did not create human robots. He created people with free will, options and the ability to choose. With a desire to be more and have more, selfishness has driven us to elicit wrong ideas and choices that lead to destruction. We simply cannot help ourselves. We want.

Through Adam, sin entered a perfect world and changed the relationship between men and women and their relationship with God forever. Sin put enmity between the sexes and broke their perfect relationship with the Creator. Adam blamed Eve and God for his sin. Eve blamed the serpent. Neither of them accepted personal responsibility for their disobedience. Because of man's role as head, sin was imputed to him and entered the world through him. Thus began the battle of the sexes and it has continued throughout the centuries creating complete havoc on marriage, family, church, community and world. Roles changed. Sexual orientation changed. The male/female relationships and roles became distorted and twisted. Man and woman became competitors. These consequences are the direct result of sin. "The significance of sin lies in the fact that it is against God, even when the wrong we do is to others or ourselves" (Unger 1988 [1957], 1198).

As a result of original sin, divorce is rampant and families have been destroyed. Mothers have been forced into the workplace, leaving children to be raised by someone else, or left alone to fend for themselves. With no father as leader of the family, these children have become products of a corrupt society. Without a male leader in the family, women and children have been exploited and demeaned, exhausted and exasperated.

Male headship was established before the fall and was not a consequence of the fall. The fall affected the destiny of man. The male/female relationship with each other and with God was severed. God's plan for humanity, however, did not change. As a result of sin, the role reversal and tensions between the sexes has entered every avenue of society, including the church. In the fight for equality, the women's equality movement placed a deeper wedge in the male/female relationship and has made life more difficult, demanding and chaotic for women. The torch of the women's right's crusade continues to burn brightly in the here and now. It has created an inaccurate distinction in the roles of men and women. No area of humanity is immune to this war of the sexes. "Being created in God's image is one of the most staggering statements in the whole Bible, yet it has become so familiar the shock of it has completely worn off" (Custis James 2005, 32). When we grasp this one extremely profound concept, it will change the way we live. We are created to embody the very character of God and through the power of the Holy Spirit, we have the ability to respond accordingly.

The Idea of Submission

Submission goes against the grain, and the grappling of it begins practically at birth. Infants obey or disobey in choosing to eat or sleep. The choices multiply exponentially as a child grows into adulthood. Submission is a learned behavior. Its practice never ceases. Every thought requires an act of submission. Submission requires humility, something of which is in short order among the human race. Although implied, obedience is the initial human behavior both taught and learned and its relentless persistence follows us to the grave. In the beginning, God the Creator, gave man a choice and with that choice, the option to choose wrongly. Of course, God desires our obedience. However, devoid of the freedom to choose, our obedience would be involuntary. God's desire is for our obedience resulting from love, adoration, worship and honor. Adam and Eve both had a choice. Eve made her choice. Adam made his, and the sentence was handed down. The consequences were irreversible. Sin brought both physical and spiritual death to the human race. Adam and Eve's fall from grace affected all of creation. Webster's Dictionary defines the word submit as to give or yield to the power or authority of another, to subject to some kind of treatment or influence, to defer to another's judgment, opinion, decision (Webster 2001, 784). Submit in the Greek New Testament means to subordinate, be under obedience, put under, subdue unto, and submit self to (NASB 1971, 75). The act of submission is not one easily accepted or practiced. Submission requires obedience. It requires a conscious continuous dying to self. "Submit yourselves, therefore to God" (James 4:7). Submit is a present tense verb indicating a habitual action that regularly occurs without interruption. The word, therefore, is inferential, meaning to derive by reasoning, to draw a conclusion to. In other words, continually submit yourselves to God because it is the reasonable thing to do. "This is a direct command and indicates the need for a decisive and urgent break from the old life" (ESV 2011, 1516). The first act of submission is to God because he is God. He is the Master Creator and creation is his by right of ownership. It all belongs to him, and he owns all rights to it. Submission is the conscious and continual act of obedience to God.

"Give thanks always and for everything to God the Father in the name of our Lord Jesus Christ, submitting to one another out of reverence to Christ" (Ephesians 5:20-21). In this context, the Apostle Paul is referring to mutual submission in personal relationships within a Christian home. This mutual submission is based on love and reverence for God. Submission is an act of worship and honor, in reverence to God in thankfulness for everything. "Wives, submit to your own husbands, as to the Lord. For the husband is the head of the wife even as Christ is the head of the Church, his body, and is himself its Savior" (Ephesians 5:22). It is easy to submit when the husband loves his wife sacrificially, as Christ loves the church. This paints a beautiful picture of a man and a woman, in a Christian home where they love each other, and both love God. Even where a Christian wife may have to stand with Christ against the sinful will of the husband, she can still have a spirit of submission - a disposition to yield. By her attitude and behavior, she can demonstrate that resisting his will is not her preference. Her demeanor can show her desire is for him to turn from sin and submit to God. As the husband assumes spiritual headship of the home, the wife can honor him without conflict.

Submission sometimes assumes incorrect implications. Several of these implications are as follows:

1. Submission does not mean putting a husband in the place of Christ.
2. Submission does not mean giving up independent thought.
3. Submission does not mean a wife should give up efforts to influence and guide her husband.
4. Submission does not mean a wife should give in to every demand of her husband.
5. Submission is not based on lesser intelligence or competence.
6. Submission does not mean being fearful or timid.
7. Submission is not inconsistent with equality in Christ. (Piper & Grudem 1991, 194-195).

Submission is an act of the obedience, beginning with a heart that is willing to submit to God.

How do we reconcile the command of submission for women who have never married? How do we reconcile this command for divorced women and widows? Where does the single woman fit into this plan? We all are to submit completely every area of our lives to God first and foremost. What is required of a single woman still living in her father's home? It has been established that the father is the head of the family. So the single woman would be under her father's leadership. If an unmarried woman is living on her own, is divorced or widowed, and a member of the body of Christ, her headship would be godly church leadership in the area of accountability, godly instruction, advice and support. By design, God intended that women never be left unprotected from the world. In every case, submission is a Christian woman's unconditional obligation as commanded by God. It is a heart condition. "Woman was created to know and walk with God and to make him known to others by reflecting his character in her life. This is a woman's true path to fulfillment and meaning – the only way we will ever discover who we are and find our purpose. And it is accessible to all of us" (Custis James 2005, 35).

Women in the Twenty-First Century Church

The Bible has been accused of contradicting itself on the position of women. "Ultimately, women's work in the church is not a gender issue but a theological matter" (Custis James 2001, 205). Scripture does not contradict Scripture. Scripture interprets Scripture. "The author of Scripture is the Holy Spirit and contradictions cannot exist; any appearance of contradiction results from the reader's lack of understanding" (Clouse 1989, 71). This fundamental truth provides the foundation for determining women's roles in the Twenty-First Century Church.

Centuries later, we have gone from clothing made of fig leaves for Adam and Eve to silk suits, stilettos and accessorizing. How do we reconcile this span of time and incredible change? There are two schools of thought on the roles of gender in the church. "Egalitarianism emphasizes 'equality' between men and women, meaning some governing and teaching roles in the church can be employed by women. Complementarianism emphasizes than men and women, while equal in value, have complementary differences meaning that some governing and teaching roles in the church are reserved for men" (Grudem 1999, 206). We have to determine what we believe. That requires careful Bible study and prayer. There are many questions to be answered. It is vital that assumptions are not based on presupposed ideas. We must determine what God says and follow in obedience. "God is the one who authorized the commandment for men to bear the primary responsibility for the family and church. If God wills for men, not women, to serve as spiritual leaders, no other reason is needed" (Sumner 2003, 279).

All things considered, where do women fit in the church today? Be encouraged by the women in Scriptures who contributed to the spread of the gospel and the building of God's kingdom. Men and women are fellow workers in ministry. Both men and women possess all the spiritual gifts. "No spiritual gift was withheld from women, including teaching and leadership. Women participated in ministry in the Scriptures, but their ministry was a complimentary and supportive ministry, a ministry that fostered and preserved male leadership in the church" (Piper & Grudem 1991, 215).

We must never underestimate the influence of godly women in the home, church, community and world. Women, in our supportive roles, have literally changed the world. The greatest role of women is that of wife and mother. Likewise, unmarried and childless women have a significant influence on men and children in ministry through support, encouragement, prayer, and service.

Women have great influence in missions, exercising talents and gifts, serving and working to preserve and advance the cause of Christ both in the church and the entire world. Women who are gifted in teaching and leadership have more than ample opportunity to do so in related roles. "There is so much to do to advance the gospel of Christ that no woman should fear that there is no place for her in ministry" (Piper & Grudem 1991, 222). Women in ministry serve to build the body of Christ so that the work of Christ can be accomplished.

Eve's legacy is one of sin and redemption. Eve's ancestry can be traced through her son, Seth. They are direct ancestors of Jesus Christ. From Eve, we learn that God has a plan for our lives and in and through him, we have the blessed hope of victory. We, the daughters of Eve, have the same choices and decisions as she. From Eve, we learn that the pleasures of sin are simply not worth the experience of a severed relationship with God. From her, we can learn that God does not have a plan B. We do not have the ability to alter God's plan. We do not have the power to abort God's plan for our lives. Nothing can separate us for the love of God that is in Christ Jesus. Sin entered a perfect world through man. God entered an imperfect, sinful world to save man from sin and its consequence. The choice is ours. A right relationship with God is our ultimate purpose. All else is inconsequential. The First Lady, Eve, exemplifies God's promises. Her sin and subsequent separation from God did not end there. She participated in God's plan for reconciliation which offers hope for all mankind through his Son, born of a woman, for whom he came to offer salvation.

"Now faith is being sure of what we hope for and certain of what we do not see." (Hebrews 11:1)

Chapter 2

The Mother of a Nation

Infertility has plagued women throughout the centuries. While the field of medicine has made great advancements in assisting infertile women to conceive children, it is an arduous journey. Infertility no longer carries the stigma it did in the ancient Old Testament. Women were created with a longing to bear and nurture children. For some, it is a desire that is never satisfied. Sarah's deep desire was satisfied at a time when least expected and quite unlikely.

Sarah was a woman in whom we can relate on many levels. She is seen at her best and her worst. In Sarah, we get the real picture and the true personhood of a woman - the good, the bad, the ugly and the loveliness that emerged. Sarah ended well and is a great example for all of us.

Her story begins in Ur of the Chaldeans in Mesopotamia, which is somewhere in modern Southern Iraq. "Sarah appears to be the only daughter of Terah and half-sister of Abraham, Nahor, and Haran (Custis James 2005, 67). Scripture reveals that Sarah became the wife of her half-brother, Abraham. Abraham said, "Besides, she is indeed my sister, the daughter of my father, though not the daughter of my mother, and she became my wife" (Genesis 20:12). While this relationship raises questions in current culture, half-sibling relationships were not considered incest in Abraham's time. While taboo today, it was quite common in ancient Israel. Abraham was a ninth generation descendant of Noah. The population was not exactly abundant.

"Through Abraham (and Sarah), God was formally launching his plan of redemption that ultimately led to Christ. Sarah's three brothers became the pillars of biblical history. These three tributaries of Terah's family went their separate ways, but reunited generations later when Abraham's male descendants (Isaac, Jacob and Boaz) married female descendants of his brothers (Rebecca, Leah, Rachel and Ruth)" (Custis James 2005, 67).

Character

Biblical accounts reveal that Sarah was extremely beautiful, which no doubt gained her favor and privilege. Centuries later, nothing has changed. Beauty continues to be valued, earning both favor and privilege. There is, however, a downside to beauty. It can affect character. Sarah's character revealed some flaws. She sometimes behaved badly. "She could throw fits and tantrums, and at times was impatient, temperamental, conniving, cantankerous, cruel, flighty, pouty, jealous, erratic, and unreasonable, a whiner, a complainer, or a nag" (MacArthur 2005, 27). The Bible does not reveal these character traits in Eve's repertoire of sin, but there is no doubt Eve demonstrated these same traits. We all do. We have Eve's sin nature. It is ingrained in us. It goes back to the will to choose and sometimes it is just easier to succumb to the sin nature and take the easy route, to our detriment. Sarah's life, however, on the whole, is characterized by humility. As we mature spiritually, we learn that godly character begets beauty.

The Move

"Now the Lord said to Abraham, 'Go from your own country and your kindred and your father's house to the land I will show you. I will make you a great nation; I will bless you and make your name great, so that you will be a blessing" (Genesis 12:1-2). While this move was surely faced with mixed emotion, Sarah loved Abraham and was devoted to him. By all accounts, she was eager to embark on this journey with him. She also faced the sorrow of leaving family and familiar surroundings, and the challenge of living a nomadic life. Abraham was quite wealthy, with an entourage of servants and herds of animals. Sarah was obviously quite capable in managing a vast household and would be a valuable asset on their journey. The trek to the land of Canaan was by no means easy or uneventful. They faced danger, famine, insecurity, and obstacles. Trials tested Sarah. However, Sarah submitted to Abraham, thereby submitting to God. "Where Abraham went, Sarah went, not as his shadow but as a strong influence. Together they experienced the vicissitudes of nomadic life and in them great spiritual significance. Sarah's love and loyalty were blessed by Abraham's devotion to her" (Deen 1983, 9).

Sarah loved God. There was no doubt that the promise made to Abraham included her, indicating that she would become the mother through whom a great nation would evolve. Sarah was sixty-five years old and Abraham seventy-five when God called them to embark on this journey.

Sarah's Barrenness

Abraham, considering his age, was obviously inquisitive concerning God's promise. Sarah was well past childbearing age. Conceiving and bearing a child at their ages would seem impossible. "And Abram said, 'Behold you have given me no offspring, and a member of my household will be my heir.' And the word of the Lord came to him: 'Your very own son shall be your heir'" (Genesis 15:3-4). It was customary for wealthy, childless couples to adopt a servant and make him their heir. Abraham's suggestion was quickly dismissed for God promised Abraham a son of his own. Sarah's excitement and joy at the prospect of becoming a mother eventually came into question as the years passed by and she was not able to conceive. She was well aware of the promise, yet doubt, fear, and unbelief clouded her understanding. "In Ancient Israel, children, and especially sons, were regarded as gifts of God, often as a reward for a righteous life. A woman who could not bear children seemed marked with divine disapproval and might well be divorced or pushed aside in disdain by a rival wife" (Pope 1994, 582).

Praying expectantly, faithfully waiting for God to move and getting no response led Sarah to despair. It is there where her doubt and questions began. "God's silence is one of the most disconcerting experiences any of his children endure. We can persevere through just about anything so long as we sense the warmth and reassurance of his presence" (Custis James 2005, 69). On the pentacle of the spiritual mountaintop, we believe anything is possible. When we begin the descent into the spiritual valley, God's faithfulness comes into question; doubt and fear creep in, and eventually the circumstances become all consuming. We question God. We question ourselves. We look inward and lament the lack we find there. It is here, where the focus turns from God to circumstances. It is here where we take matters into our own hands. "And Sarai said to Abram, 'The Lord has prevented me from bearing children. Go into my servant; it may be that I shall obtain children by her.' And Abram listened to the voice of Sarai" (Genesis 16:2). In ancient Middle Eastern custom, surrogates were common and in the case of barren wives and children born of that union became the property of the barren wife. This practice was purely cultural but contrary to God's design for monogamous marriages. Seeing the whole picture, it is difficult to understand the unfaithfulness of both Sarah and Abraham. Yet, we are no different when it comes to our own circumstances. We, too, take matters into our hands and in like manner, suffer the consequences of our impatience and unbelief. How often we miss enormous blessings in our haste to force God's hand. The birth of Ishmael, the child born of Abraham and Hagar (Sarah's servant and surrogate), invoked conflict.

"Sarah reminds us how hard it is to trust God when everything is going wrong, and all hope is lost. The forces that assault our faith can be fierce and even the strongest can stumble and fall. But in the end Sarah's faith will be stronger and have deeper roots because of all she suffered" (Custis James 2005, 71). When Sarah was ninety years of age and Abraham one hundred, a son was conceived. "The Lord visited Sarah as he had said and the Lord did to Sarah as he has promised. And Sarah conceived and bore Abraham a son in his old age at the time of which God had spoken to him" (Genesis 21:1-2). Isaac, the long awaited heir of promise was born. Sarah became the first matriarch of what became the Jewish nation. Sarah offers an exemplary example of hope. God made a promise. In spite of Sarah and all that occurred in her life, God fulfilled his promise. Sarah and Abraham show us a picture of love and devotion to each other. Even through trials and tribulations, they remained faithful.

Sarah is recognized in the New Testament as an example of submission. "For this is how the holy women of

God adorn themselves by submitting to their own husbands, as Sarah obeyed Abraham, calling him lord. And you are her children, if you do good and do not fear anything that is frightening" (1 Peter 3:5-6). "A wife's submission to her husband is more like the submission of Christ to God the Father, the submission of one to another who is equal in importance and essence" (Piper & Grudem 1991, 196).

What submission means:

1. Submission is an inner quality of gentleness that affirms the leadership of the husband.
2. Submission involves obedience like Sarah's.
3. Submission acknowledges authority that is not totally mutual (Piper & Grudem 1991, 196-198).
4. Submission is an act of the will, a heart condition and is required of all people.

The example of Sarah's obedience would be an appropriate encouragement to women, for Sarah became the mother of all God's people in the Old Covenant, even though there had been many times in which following Abraham had meant trusting God in uncertain, and even dangerous situations. "Peter says believing women are now her children (or daughters), the true members of her spiritual family. To be Sarah's daughter is to be joint heir of the promises and honor given to her and to Abraham" (Piper & Grudem 1991, 201).

A Word on the Abrahamic Covenant

"Now the Lord said to Abram, 'Go from your country and your kindred and your father's house to the land that I will show you. And I will make you a great nation, and I will bless you and make your name great, so that you will be a blessing. I will bless those who bless you, and him who dishonors you, I will curse, and in you all the families of the earth shall be blessed'" (Genesis 12:1-3). Abraham was the recipient of a covenant involving not only himself, but his posterity, natural as well as spiritual (Unger 1985 [1957], 14). The sign of the covenant was circumcision symbolizing a physical commitment to God. "You shall be circumcised in the flesh of your foreskin and it shall be a sign of the covenant between me and you…Every male throughout your generations, whether born in your house or bought with your money from any foreigner who is not your offspring shall surely be circumcised" (Genesis 17:11-13). There are two significant implications here. Gentile acceptance into the family of God was established with the Abrahamic Covenant. It was not an afterthought in the New Testament when God sent Paul to the Gentiles after the Jews rejected the gospel (Acts 18:5-8).

It appears that women were excluded from the covenant. Obviously, women cannot be circumcised. The answer to this dilemma is evident. "I (God) will bless her (Sarah), and moreover, give you a son by her. I will bless her, and she shall become nations; kings of peoples will come from her" (Genesis 17:15-16). This covenant could not be consummated without Sarah. God's command to Adam and Eve to be fruitful and multiply involved childbirth. Life could not continue in the absence of women. This makes women absolute essential parties in the fulfillment of God's plan. Therefore, the Abrahamic Covenant included women. When God orchestrated his covenant with Abraham, he provided for all peoples, men, women, Jews, and Gentiles.

There is another aspect to circumcision. Circumcision is figurative. "Circumcise therefore, the foreskin of the heart and be no longer stubborn" (Deuteronomy 10:16). "Circumcision is used as a symbol of purity of heart. Christians are said to be circumcised in Christ" (Unger 1988 [1957], 239). Symbolically, every believer's act of submission and obedience to God is a spiritual act of circumcision. God's people are called to be separated from the world. "I appeal to you therefore, brothers, by the mercies of God, to present your bodies as a living sacrifice, holy and acceptable to God, which is your spiritual worship. Do not be conformed to this world, but be transformed by the renewal of your mind, that by testing you may discern what is the will of God, what is good and acceptable and perfect" (Romans 12:1-2).

Believing women are the physical daughters of Eve and the spiritual daughters of Sarah. What can we learn from Sarah? We see her at her best and her worst. We see her become consumed with the circumstances of her barrenness to the point of despair. We see her tired of waiting for God and take matters into her own hands. We see her failures and her triumphs. We wonder how Sarah could ever have doubted God. Yet, knowing Sarah's story, we do the same thing. We get consumed with circumstances, and our focus moves from God to self. The most difficult thing for us to do is to wait in silence. We pray, hope, and wait and nothing changes. We remain faithful and God does not respond. We have three choices. We grow impatient, get ahead of God and take matters into our own hands. That never turns out well. We despair, get depressed and downtrodden and wallow in self-pity affecting our physical, emotional and spiritual health. There is no hope in doubt and faithlessness. We can trust that God is faithful and believe that nothing is too difficult for him. Regardless of what we perceive, we can trust that the all-knowing, all-powerful, all-sufficient God of all Creation has our backs. Nothing is too big or too difficult for God.

Hagar

We would be remiss in ignoring Hagar's contribution to our understanding and confirmation of the value of women in God's economy. Hagar was an Egyptian slave who belonged to Abraham and served Sarah as her handmaid. Nothing is written about Hagar's history prior to joining Abraham's clan. It is assumed she joined Abraham's entourage when they traveled through Egypt. It stands to reason that it was a difficult adjustment, having left her family, homeland and all that was familiar to enter into slavery to serve people she did not know in surroundings and a lifestyle she was unfamiliar with. Sarah's frustration in her failure to conceive and bear a child, led her to insist that Abraham sleep with Hagar so that she would conceive and bear a child that by law would become Sarah's own child.

"So, after Abram lived ten years in the land of Canaan, Sarai, Abram's wife, took Hagar the Egyptian, her servant and gave her to Abram her husband as a wife. And he went into Hagar and she conceived" (Genesis 16:3-4). Hagar conceived and the relationship between her and Sarah abruptly changed. Hagar became contemptuous. Sarah became jealous and abusive. And Sarah said to Abraham, "May the wrong that has been done to me be on you. I gave my servant to your embrace, and when she conceived, she looked on me with contempt" (Genesis 16:5). "Abram said to Sarai, 'Behold, your servant is in your power, do to her as you please.' Then Sarah dealt harshly with her and she (Hagar) fled from her" (Genesis 16:6). As if being in slavery were not degrading enough, Hagar was sent to Abraham for the purpose of impregnation. She successfully conceived a child as was planned by Sarah. At this point, all that had transpired was beyond Hagar's control. Hagar's response of contempt for her mistress, however, was an act of willful sin. The result was condemnation and abuse from her mistress. Hagar found herself in an impossible situation. In desperation to escape the situation, Hagar fled into the wilderness.

Hagar, the Egyptian slave who was forced to have sexual relations with her master, became pregnant. In showing willful contempt for Sarah, she subsequently found herself being treated harshly, and she ran away. Alone and afraid in the wilderness, Hagar encountered God. "The Angel of the Lord said to her, 'Return to your mistress and submit to her. I will surely multiply your offspring so that they cannot be numbered for multitude'"

(Genesis 16:9-10). The insignificant woman, as a result of her own willful sin, was banished into the wilderness, and was all alone with no hope. And God showed up in a big way.

"The Angel of the Lord (Jehovah) is the Lord Jesus Christ in reincarnate appearance. A study of the passages in which he is mentioned makes it clear that he is God, and that he is the second person of the Trinity. The word translated *Angel* in both Testaments mean 'messenger'; He is the '*Messenger*' of Jehovah" (McDonald 1995, 270-271). There are four convincing arguments that the Angel of the Lord referred to in the Old Testament references Deity.

1. The Second Person is the Visible God of the New Testament.
2. The Angel of Jehovah of the Old Testament no longer appears after the incarnation of Christ.
3. Both the Angel of Jehovah and Christ are sent by the Father.
4. The Angel of Jehovah could not be either the Father or the Holy Spirit (MacDonald 1995, 271).

Christ was not created. He is the person of the Trinity through whom God created the universe. Christ was with God in the beginning. This Christ spoke to Hagar, a woman of low regard, a woman of no significance. Hagar was an Egyptian, a slave, a Gentile. "Hagar's story levels a devastating blow against anyone who tried to make the case that women do not count, or we are second-class citizens in God's kingdom. God simply could not have made a stronger statement of how much he values women and how central we are to what he is doing" (Custis James 2005, 98).

In the wilderness, the Angel of God commanded Hagar to return and submit to her mistress. Submit in this context means to yield (Vine 1996, [1984], 607). The act of submission is an express command to be applied to authority on all levels. Complete submission to God results in submission to all authority, whether in the family relationship, church relationship, work relationship, or government relationship. Submission is all inclusive.

Hope for Women in the Twenty-First Century Church

All women have highs and lows. Sarah certainly had hers. We can relate to her on many levels and we can be encouraged. With all of Sarah's failures, she ended well. She persevered. Regardless of Sarah's disobedience, God was faithful. We can conclude that God's plan will be accomplished. No one is powerful enough to thwart God's will. Neither does he need our help. As we saw with Sarah, interfering in disobedience, impatience, and faithlessness only served to cause grief and pain for all concerned, including the child Hagar bore Abram. Some lessons are hard learned. The point is that the lessons are learned and serve to draw us nearer to God. No matter what life throws at us, we can stand in firm assurance that God the Father is in complete control and his plan will not fail, in spite of us.

Sarah's story has a significant effect on those women who believe the lie that the consequences of past sins result in their having missed God's plan for their lives. Christ's death on the cross conquered sin completely, with no exceptions. No sin is beyond the capacity of Christ's complete accomplishment on the cross. Christ's act on the cross defeated death, abolishing sin and guilt. Wallowing in guilt is dishonoring to God and infers that Christ's work on the cross was not enough. Forgiveness is complete in Christ.

"We demolish arguments and every pretense that sets itself up against the knowledge of God, and we take captive every thought to make it obedient to Christ." (2Corinthians 10:5)

Chapter 3

Female Prophets

Prophecy is divine revelation given directly from God to a particular recipient purposefully chosen by God. Prophecy, divine revelation, ceased at the end of the written book of Revelation. "I warn everyone who hears the words of the prophecy of this book: If anyone adds anything to them, God will add to him the plagues described in this book, and if anyone takes words away from the book of prophecy, God will take his share in the tree of life and in the holy city, which are described in this book" (Revelation 22:18-19). Biblical prophecy is ascribed exclusively to the Bible, where it began and ended. Both men and women of the Bible were recipients of direct prophecy. To whom God chose to reveal his divine revelation was his by will.

Prophecy in itself is no longer an active occurrence initiated by God in disclosing new revelation. The Bible is God's direct revelation from beginning to end. Any claim to having received a new revelation is utter fallacy. Post-Biblical revelation is revealed through God's Word by the inspiration of the Holy Spirit.

The Old Testament applied the title Prophetess to five women: Deborah, Miriam, Huldah, the wife of Isaiah, and No-adiah, a false prophetess who opposed Nehemiah. "Rabbinical tradition recognized seven prophetesses who prophesied to Israel: Sarah, Miriam, Deborah, Hannah, Abigail, Huldah, and Esther" (Bromiley 1986, 1004). Prophet means one who speaks forth openly, a proclaimer of a divine message (Vine 1996 [1984], 493). Although these women were prophetesses and leaders, they remained within the bounds of God's order of headship.

Judges Chapter 2 provides the background for the book of Judges. God brought his people out of Egypt and led them to the land of Canaan, fulfilling his covenant with them. God commanded his people not to cohabit with the pagan Canaanites who populated the land. Israel disobeyed and bowed to the gods of the Canaanites. Because of their disobedience, God allowed them to suffer the consequences. "The disobedience of the Israelites would become the means whereby God would bring them to a deeper understanding of the election purpose and a deeper understanding of his relationship to Israel. The testing will demonstrate the truth that Yahweh is faithful to the covenant even though his people are not" (LaSor, Hubbard, Bush 1987, 214). Nothing we do or fail to do can alter God's plan. He will succeed. We either choose to get on board and get involved where he is working, or we sit on the sidelines. If the focus is on Christ, the desire will be to honor and glorify him. Ours is to serve Christ the Lord with the gifts, talents and abilities he has given us. Anything otherwise is utter disobedience.

Deborah

Deborah was a prophetess and a judge who obediently served God. She was the wife of Lappidoth. Not much is known about him otherwise. For whatever reason, God included this information. Perhaps for us to realize Deborah was a godly married woman, we can determine that she was obedient to her husband's headship. Deborah had a strong relationship with God. She was a woman of prayer and faith. She was open and available for God's purpose, and God used her to deliver his people.

The term "judge" in this respect can be misleading. These individuals, except on rare occasions, are not at all like the modern concept of a judge. Normally they did not hold court, nor was their main task to hear complaints or make legal decisions. "The elders of the family usually did so in the social sphere, while priests were the final interpreters of religious law" (LaSor, Hubbard, Bush 1987, 214).

As a result of their disobedience, the Israelites were under the oppression of the Canaanites for twenty years. They found themselves facing the Canaanite army which was well prepared to recapture the land. With nowhere else to turn, the Israelites cried out to God. Deborah was the means through which God responded.

"Concerning Deborah, we are told that she was intimately acquainted with God; she was a prophetess, one that was instructed in divine knowledge by the immediate inspiration of the Holy Spirit and had gifts of wisdom to which she attained not in any ordinary way. That she was entirely devoted to the service of Israel, and perhaps being a woman; she was more easily permitted by the oppressor to do it" (Henry 1984, 139). From this, we can determine that Deborah's role was solely devoted to spiritual matters. Deborah's reputation was apparent as the Israelites sought Deborah for her intercession in prayer on their behalf for deliverance from the enemy.

Deborah received a word from the Lord that a man named Barak was to lead Israel into victory in battle against the Canaanite army. At Barak's request, Deborah accompanied him to the battlefield. "Deborah is not asserting leadership for herself; she gives priority to a man" (Piper & Grudem 1991, 216). The victory was accomplished through both Deborah and Barak. Together, God used them to save the Israelite nation. God was the orchestrator. Deborah was the instigator, Barak was the initiator. This effort could not have been successful without both participants equally supportive of the other. Deborah exercised her gift differently than the male prophets in the Old Testament. "She used to sit under the palm of Deborah between Ramah and Bethel in the hill country of Ephraim and the people of Israel came up to her for judgment" (Judges 4:5). This indicates that her prophetic instruction was done in private, an additional confirmation of God's preservation of male headship. Male prophets proclaimed the word of God publicly.

Miriam

"Then Joseph died, and all his brothers and all that generation. But the people of Israel were fruitful and increased greatly; they multiplied and grew exceedingly strong, so that the land was filled with them. Now there arose a new king over Egypt, who did not know Joseph" (Exodus 1:6-8). Pharaoh became fearful that the Israelites were a threat to the kingdom, so he made them slaves and oppressed them. Even under harsh oppression, the Israelites continued to grow in number. Pharaoh instigated a plot to have all the male newborns killed. Moses was born during that period. In an effort to protect him from impending death, his mother hid him in a basket among the reeds along the bank of the Nile River. There, Moses' older sister, Miriam watched over him. Pharaoh's daughter found Moses floating in the river, and Miriam intervened, saving his life. Years later, Miriam became one of the more well-known prophetesses, although largely due to her association with Moses. She, with her brothers, Moses and Aaron was an influential member of the Exodus leadership. She was the first woman in the Old Testament to be given the title Prophetess.

When the Israelites were finally allowed to leave Egypt, they crossed the Red Sea on dry land. Regretting his decision to let them go, Pharaoh's army pursued them into the sea where they all drowned. Exodus 15 introduces the Song of Moses and Miriam, sung in praise and thankfulness to the Lord for his protection and salvation from Pharaoh's army. "Then Miriam the prophetess, Aaron's sister, took a tambourine in her hand, and all the women followed her with tambourines and dancing" (Exodus 15:20). This verse is significant in understanding Miriam's roll in ministry. According to Exodus 15:20, Miriam led women. As a prophetess and leader, Miriam was under the headship of

Moses, and her roles in ministry were in combination with and complementary to Moses' ministry. Her ministry role did not include teaching Scripture or leading men.

Huldah

There is not an abundance of information on Huldah. Her brief appearance is found in 2 Kings 22:14-20 and 2 Chronicles 34:22-29. She lived in Jerusalem during the reign of Josiah.

The Book of the Law had been discovered and read to Josiah. "And when the king heard the words of the Book of the Law, he tore his clothes…Go inquire of the Lord for me and for the people, and for all Judah, concerning the words of this book that has been found. For great is the wrath of the Lord that is kindled against us because our fathers have not obeyed the words of this book, to do according to all that is written concerning us" (2 Kings 22:11-13).

Her reputation as a woman of God led seekers to her to obtain a word from the Lord. This indicates her obedience to him would have been manifested in her submission to him. "So Hilkiah the priest, and Ahikam, and Achbor, and Shaphan, and Asaiah went to Huldah the prophetess, the wife of Shallum the son of Tikvah, son of Harhas, keeper of the wardrobe, and they talked with her" (2 Kings 22:14). She revealed all that God had spoken to her concerning the disaster that he would bring on Judah because they had forsaken him and followed other gods. "And they brought back word to the king that because of his penitent and humble heart he would not see the disaster that God would bring" (2 Kings 22: 20b).

Although it was rare for God to speak through women, he did so. However, there is no evidence that these women taught Scripture to men or were leaders of men. They were within the bounds of God's design for headship.

Isaiah's Wife

"Of all the prophets of Israel, Isaiah stands out as incomparably the greatest and has commonly been referred to as the evangelical prophet. Not much is known about Isaiah. However, Isaiah was married and designated his wife a prophetess" (Bromiley 1986, 855). Isaiah said, "And I went to the prophetess and she conceived and bore a son" (Isaiah 8:3). Perhaps she was designated as a prophetess simply because she was the wife of a prophet. As in all cases of prophetesses, there is no evidence of her ever teaching Scriptures to men or directly leading men. This supports God's design of headship based on the Genesis account of Adam and Eve.

Anna

Anna appears briefly in the New Testament. Luke 2:36-38 describes Anna as the daughter of Phanuel of the tribe of Asher. Asher was the eighth son of Jacob, and he was the second born to Zilpah, the slave of Leah (Pope 1994, 49). Anna married early in life and became widowed after seven years. "From that time to the age of eighty-four, she never left the temple, serving night and day with fasting and prayer" (Luke 2:37). "Probably due to her devotion to God in her great faith and holiness, she was allowed to live in one of the chambers of the women's court. Anna belonged to the remnant. She was a woman who listened to the readings of the scrolls of the sacred Scriptures and believed fully in the prophecies they contained. Not only did she believe, but she watched unceasingly for the coming Messiah" (Deen 1955, 174). She gave her entire life in service and worship of Jehovah. Her days were filled with an all-consuming hunger for God. Luke refers to Anna as a prophetess. Prophetess in the Greek New Testament means inspired woman. Inspired in this sense refers to illumination. "Illumination is a ministry of the Holy Spirit that enables all who are in right relationship with God to understand the objective written in revelation" (Unger 1988 [1957], 621).

Mary and Joseph took Jesus to Jerusalem to present him to the Lord, according to the Law of Moses, and to offer a sacrifice. "Now there was a man in Jerusalem whose name was Simeon, an elderly prophet, who was righteous and devout. And it had been revealed to him by the Holy Spirit that he would not see death before he had seen the Lord Jesus Christ" (Luke 2:25-26). "And he came in the Spirit into the temple, and when the parents brought Jesus into the temple, Simeon praised God saying, 'Now I may depart in peace, according to your word, my eyes have seen your salvation'" (Luke 2:27-30). Anna was among the first witnesses who knew and understood the significance of the birth of Christ. "And coming up at that very hour she began to give thanks to God and to speak of him to all who were waiting for the redemption of Jerusalem" (Luke 2:38). Anna's inclusion in Luke's gospel indicates the importance of her life and testimony. Her testimony remains a great example and witness to all who read of her life. Nothing, however, in this passage indicates that Anna had a priority position in the Temple or that she was a teacher of Scriptures or leader of men.

Women in the Twenty-First Century

How do we address women in management roles in the business world in the Twenty-First Century? How are we to view female officers in civic organizations? First, the world is not commanded to follow God's standards for his people. God's standards are for his church. Christian women are called according to God's purpose. "Now, with over half the women in the United States in the labor force and with many households headed by a woman, the whole concept of what a woman does and what a man does is changing. The idyllic picture of the nuclear family-a working father, homemaking mother and two or more children-may persist in people's minds but constitutes less than six percent of households in the United States" (Clouse 1989, 232). Equality continues to be hard-pressed in every aspect. Both the feminist movement and economic necessity has placed women in almost every job traditionally held by men (Clouse 1989, 232). The result, rape and abuse of women in the work force have escalated, and the family unit suffers. Women continue to pay a huge price for insisting on entering fields of work that are simply not suitable for women. Men and women are different, emotionally, physically, and better suited for different roles. Crossing gender roles in any area is problematic for both men and women. Equality continues to be a problematic topic in the Twenty-First Century. Each one of us women has been assigned a huge task. In following in obedience, there is no occasion to entertain conflict. Time will not allow lament over what women cannot do.

Women in the Twenty-First Century church have all the same talents and gifts distributed to our male counterparts. We all have a place in the kingdom, and our act of worship is to fulfill the call on our lives to serve and honor God. We are called to submit in obedience first to God and his order in headship. Nothing in Scripture violates that order. The opposite of order is chaos. Left with no restrictions, humanity will push the proverbial envelope to the point of self-destruction.

"Our society needs the influence and action of Christian women. Women will be used as instruments of healing and peacemakers, fixers of the world, able to bring people together, to help mend relationships. Women are key players in God's plan for the present age" (Piper & Grudem 1991, 395). Anna's story reveals to us when we have a right relationship with God, living wholly for him and making him Lord of our lives, he will reveal himself to us through his Word. When all else takes a back seat to our relationship with God, he responds by giving us a deeper understanding of his word and how it applies to our lives.

"Consider it pure joy, my brothers, whenever you face trials of many kinds, because you know that the testing of your faith develops perseverance." (James 1:2-3)

Chapter Four

Sister Wives

While Polygamy is illegal in the United States, it is practiced, though rarely, among some in the fundamental Mormon belief. Polygamy is not a new concept. It was common in the ancient Old Testament. God did not ordain it, and its practice never met with his approval. Polygamy was a departure from the law. It was tolerated because of the hardness of hearts of the Israelites. It continues to be tolerated today.

Through a series of events, Jacob, the son of Isaac and Rebecca, deceived his father into receiving the family blessing reserved for the first born son, his brother Esau. To protect Jacob from Esau's retaliation, Rebecca convinced Isaac to send him to live with her brother Laban in Haran.

When Jacob neared Haran, he encountered his beautiful young cousin, Rachel, tending her father Laban's flock and immediately fell in love with her (Gardener 1994, 175). Subsequently, Jacob was accepted into Laban's clan. Jacob made an agreement with Laban to work for him seven years for Rachel's hand in marriage. He was, however, duped into marrying Rachel's sister, Leah. A week later, he married Rachel as well. The twelve tribes of Israel emerged from this polygamous relationship.

Rachel

"Now Laban had two daughters; the name of the older was Leah, and the name of the younger, Rachel. And Leah's eyes were weak, but Rachel was beautiful of form and face. Now Jacob loved Rachel, so he said (to Laban), 'I will serve you seven years for your younger daughter, Rachel'" (Genesis 29:16-17). Seven years later the deceiver is deceived. "According to custom, it was arranged that the bride should go into the groom on the wedding night, veiled and perhaps when the room was in darkness" (MacDonald 1990, 65). It was the local custom that the older daughters marry before the younger and Laban arranged for Leah to take Rachel's place. Unsuspecting Jacob consummated his marriage with the wrong sister. Leah desperately yearned for Jacob's favor. Even the birth of coveted sons by Leah did not diminish Jacob's love for Rachel.

"According to Biblical record, Jacob's union with Rachel was celebrated at the close of Leah's marriage festivities, lasting for about a week. Jacob, however, had to serve another seven years as a shepherd, making fourteen altogether, for his beloved Rachel" (Deen 1983, 30). Leah bore three sons while Rachel was unable to conceive. Like Sarah and Rebecca, Rachel was barren. "When Rachel saw that she bore Jacob no children, she envied her sister" (Genesis 30:1). Rachel, in her desperation, gave her maid

Bilhah as a surrogate to Jacob. Bilhah bore Rachel two sons, Dan and Naphtali. These sons did not satisfy Rachel's desire to bear children of her own. "Now it was in the days of the wheat harvest that Reuben (Leah's first born) went and found mandrakes in the field and brought them to his mother" (Genesis 30:14). Rachel asked her sister for some of the mandrakes. "But she (Leah) said, 'Is it a small matter that you have taken away my husband? Would you take away my son's mandrakes also?' Rachel said, 'Then he (Jacob) may lie with you tonight in exchange for your son's mandrakes'" (Genesis 30:15).'" This exchange between Rachel and Leah implies that Rachel had control by having given Leah permission to lie with Jacob. The mandrakes were evidently a crucial commodity. Because of the rivalry between the sisters it seems Rachel would oppose any opportunity for Leah to conceive again. Rachel believed the exchange would be in her favor. "From the most ancient time, aphrodisiac virtues have been ascribed to the mandrake, which was therefore supposed to cure barrenness. The plant's root was esteemed as a love medicine" (Deen1983, 32). "Mandrake is the common name for members of the plant genus Mandragora, particularly the species Mandragora officinarum, belonging to the nightshades family (Solanaceae). Because mandrake contains deliriant hallucinogenic tropane alkaloids such as atropine, scopolamine, apoatropine, and hyoscyamine, and the roots sometimes contain bifurcations causing them to resemble human figures, their roots have long been used in magic rituals, today also in contemporary pagan traditions such as Wicca and Odinism" (Piccillo, Mondati, Moro 2002). Rachel appeared to have a propensity for mystic solutions rather than dependence upon God.

"When Jacob came in from the field in the evening, Leah went out to meet him and said, 'You must come in to me, for I have hired you with my son's mandrakes'" (Genesis 30:16). Jacob laid with Leah, and she conceived and bore a fifth son. The mandrakes did not provide the anticipated solution to Rachel's barrenness. It was after Leah had given birth to her sixth son and a daughter, that Rachel conceived her first child, Joseph. Although, Jacob's favor of Joseph and Joseph's mishandling of his favor with God caused great conflict within the family, Joseph was among those who displayed the most Christ-like character in the Old Testament.

After Joseph's birth, Jacob yearned for his homeland. Jacob consulted Rachel and Leah, demonstrating that he, like other patriarchs, took no major steps without counseling from his wives (Deen 1983, 33). Rachel and Leah agreed on the departure. While his father-in-law was away, Jacob left with all that belonged to him to go to the land of Canaan to his father Isaac. Before departing and unbeknownst to Jacob, Rachel stole her father's household idols. "Laban had gone to shear his sheep, and Rachel stole her father's household gods" (Genesis 31:19). "Possession of these household gods may have implied leadership of the family; and in the case of a married daughter, assured her husband the right to her father's property. Laban had sons of his own and they alone had the right to their father's teraphim" (MacDonald 1989, 67). Rachel's theft was a serious matter. Rachel may have also believed the idols might bring some kind of protection. This would offer further evidence of Rachel's interest or belief in idolatry. When Laban learned of Jacob's departure, he and his men pursued and overtook him. Laban, confronted Jacob and accused him of stealing his family household gods. Laban made a thorough search of the caravan, but did not find the idols. Rachel had hidden the gods in her camel's saddle. "Rachel excused herself for not getting off the camel's saddle to honor her father because it was her menstrual period – or so she said" (McDonald 1989, 67). This indicates Rachel was unclean, according to custom, so

Laban would not have pressed the issue. Laban departed without his idols. They remained in Rachel's possession.

Jacob returned to Canaan and God commanded him to go to Bethel. "So Jacob said to his household and all who were with him, 'Put away your foreign gods that are among you and purify yourselves and change your garments. Then let us arise and go up to Bethel so that I may make there an alter to God'" (Genesis 35:2-3). The family gave to Jacob all the foreign gods they had and he buried them; however such idols turned up on a number of occasions in subsequent history. "It appears that throughout much of their history, the Israelites did not find possession of teraphim inconsistent with Yahwism. They are spoken of with disapproval from the time of Samuel (1 Samuel 7:3) to that of Zechariah" (Zechariah 10:2) (Tenney 1976 [1975], 677). It is probable that Rachel's father's household gods were among those surrendered to Jacob, indicating her repentance and submission to God.

The Israelites continued to possess foreign gods. Whether or not the idols were worshipped, ownership of them demonstrated disobedience to God. "You shall have no other gods before me. You shall not make a carved image, or any likeness of anything that is in heaven above, or that is in the earth beneath or that is in the waters under the earth. You shall not bow down to them or serve them, for I am your God" (Exodus 20:5a). Idols, however, are not always visible to the naked eye. Idols take on many forms.

The journey of Jacob's family to Bethlehem was not without difficulty. "When they were still some distance from Ephrath, Rachel went into labor. And when her labor was the hardest, the midwife said to her, 'Do not fear, for you have another son.' And her soul was departing (for she was dying), she called his name Benoni; but his father called him Benjamin" (Genesis 35:16-18). Rachel was the first woman recorded in the Bible to die in childbirth, leaving behind the children she coveted and the husband who loved her. While her honors and blessings were many, Rachel's discontentment seemed to plague most of her life. We can only speculate as to why death visited her so soon after realizing her deepest desire to bear children.

Leah

Leah was older but the lesser of the sisters in beauty, desire and in love. She was abundantly blessed by God in her fertility. Leah was resentful and jealous of her sister, Rachel. Leah did not possess her husband's love. But Leah was more fortunate than her younger sister in one important respect. "When the Lord saw that Leah was hated, he opened her womb. She bore Jacob six sons and a daughter, while her maid Zilpah bore two additional sons (Gad and Asher) to Jacob (which also counted as hers) before Rachel was able to have sons of her own" (Pope 1994, 269). With each of the births of her first three sons, she hoped to earn the love of her husband. Yet she failed.

"And she conceived again and bore a son, Judah, and said, 'This time I will praise the Lord'" (Genesis 29:35). With this birth, she recognized God's blessings in her children. She, however, continued to fall short in the competition for the love of her husband.

Leah survived Rachel. She assumed the coveted position of chief wife and she and Jacob lived long lives together. Leah's sons were Reuben, Simeon, Levi, Judah, Issachar, Zebulun ancestors of half the tribes of Israel. Zilpah, Leah's maidservant, bore two additional sons to Jacob, Gad, and Asher. Leah also bore one daughter, Dinah. "From Leah's son Judah came the tribe of Judah, from which came the line of Boaz, Jesse, and David, and the Messiah. And from her son Levi sprang the priesthood" (Deen 1983, 36). Leah appears in the genealogy of Jesus, giving her the greatest honor among the sisters.

Concubines

"The practice of concubinage began early in Genesis and became common practice almost limited to the period of the patriarchs, conquests, and early kingdom. A concubine was slave woman in ancient societies who was the legal chattel of her master. She was not free and did not have the rights of the free wife. Her children would become co-heirs with the children of the wife" (Tenney 1976 [1975], 935). Concubines were absorbed into the families. This practice of concubines was not instituted by God. "In the process of time concubinage appears to have degenerated into a regular custom among the Jews, and the institutions of Moses were directed to prevent excess abuse by wholesome laws and regulations" (Exodus 21:7-9, Deuteronomy 21:10-14). Christianity restored the sacred institution of marriage and concubinage was ranked with fornication and adultery.

Children of Dysfunctional Families

The families of Adam, Abraham, Isaac and Jacob were filled with discord. Children born to these families harbored ill will, and sibling rivalry was problematic. In Jacob's case, there was double jeopardy. He not only had two wives, but two concubines, and children with all of them. The children of these families effected severe conflict.

With Adam and Eve, their eldest son Cain killed his younger brother, Abel, out of envy. Sarah gave her servant Hagar to Abraham as a surrogate. Hagar became pregnant and gave birth to Ishmael. Both Hagar and Ishmael were rejected by Sarah and Abraham. Isaac, the son of Abraham and Sarah, married Rebecca. While there were no recorded concubines or additional wives, there was discord among their twin sons. Esau was favored by Isaac, Jacob was favored by Rebecca. Esau sold his birthright to Jacob.

Jacob deceived Isaac and received Esau's blessing. Jacob fled in fear of reprisal from Esau and his relocation to Haran resulted in his never seeing his mother again. She died while he was away. Jacob, the son of Isaac and Rebecca, had two wives and two concubines, twelve sons and a daughter with the four women. The Bible describes discord, discontent and sinful acts of violence among the siblings of these unions. Sin continues to be the ultimate destroyer of the family unit.

Twenty-First Century Families

Today, in the Twenty-First Century, the model family unit has become distorted. Single parent families are now headed by women who are responsible for the home and children, holding down full-time jobs and juggling relentless responsibilities. Many of these children are being raised without a father in the picture. "One in three children being raised without a father is due in part by a growing trend of children born outside of marriage. Approximately fifteen million children live without a father" (Nye 2012). Absentee fathers have become the norm. The results have proven to be extremely devastating to children and society as a whole.

Research shows when a child is raised in a father-absent home, he or she is:

1. Four times more likely to live in poverty
2. More likely to suffer emotional and behavioral problems
3. Two times greater risk of infant mortality
4. More likely to go to prison
5. More likely to commit crime
6. Seven times more likely to become pregnant as a teen
7. More likely to face abuse and neglect
8. More likely to abuse drugs and alcohol
9. Two times more likely to suffer obesity
10. Two times more likely to drop out of high school (Sanders 2013)

We can predict a higher divorce rate when the criteria of success in marriage changes from devotion to family, integrity, security and commitment to that of personal gratification, the need to feel validated, when compromise is deemed to be a sign of weakness, and when doing your own thing and getting yours are justified. A higher divorce rate is inevitable when divorce is easy to obtain, when the negative costs of commitment are emphasized, when selfishness is idealized as autonomy. When moral responsibility is to the self rather than the relationship, divorce increases. Commitment involves not only mutual feeling but also interdependent obligation. The breakdown of the family unit has affected children in life altering ways.

With several women of the ancient Old Testament all-consuming heartaches revolved around the inability to bear children. The inability to bear children continues to be a problem for some women today. It is ironic that in the Twenty-First Century aborting unwanted babies has become ordinary. Consider abortion, Planned Parenthood, and a woman's right to choose. The law of the land gives women the legal right to discard the life of an unborn fetus at will. Women were created to bear and mother children. Disrupting the cycle of life disrupts a woman's physical, emotional and intellectual psyche. Beware of the lies that reveal partial truths. Abortion is legalized murder.

In today's culture, sin has acquired a new definition. In our ensuing politically correct society, tolerance has become the new standard. In many churches, addressing sin is considered offensive, and it is no longer confronted or even referenced. This justification has resulted in a culture that demands acceptance and approval for deviant behaviors. Divorce, alcoholism, drug abuse, promiscuity, children born out of wedlock, homosexuality, child molestation, domestic abuse, abortion, perverted morals, ethics, and values are sinful behaviors that continue to plague our society. Sin has become a justifiable act that enables offenders to continue behaviors that force incredible sufferings on individuals, families, and society as a whole.

Lives of happiness and ease are allusive. Answers are not promised to questions nor are solutions to all problems. Freedom from trials and tribulations are not assured. Rather, we are told to expect them. "Count it all joy, my brothers, when you meet trials of various kinds, for you know that the testing of your faith produces steadfastness. And let steadfastness have its full effect, that you may be perfect and complete, lacking nothing" (James 1:2). Life is painful. It is in the painful moments that we seek God. When everything around is spiraling into oblivion, God is the firm foundation. Our purpose is to know God. He allows suffering and heartache because in the darkest hours, we seek him. When faith is hanging by a thread and hope seems lost, God is able. We are vision impaired. Our view of life is based on perception. God sees the whole picture, and whether or not it feels like it, he has our best interests in mind. "Therefore, since we are surrounded by so great a cloud of witnesses, let us also lay aside every weight and sin which clings so closely, and let us run with endurance the race that is set before us, looking to Jesus the founder and perfecter of our faith, who endured the cross, despising the shame, and is seated at the right hand of the throne of God" (Hebrews 12:1-2). We must trust in God's sovereignty. To effect change, we must repent of sin and surrender all to Jesus. The ultimate goal is to become like the One in whose likeness we were created.

"Dear friends, do not be surprised at the painful trial you are suffering, as though something strange were happening to you. But rejoice that you participate in the sufferings of Christ, so that you may be overjoyed when his glory is revealed" (1 Peter 4:12-13)

Chapter 5

In-Laws

"In the days when the judges ruled there was a famine in the land (Israel), and a man of Bethlehem in Judah went to sojourn in the country of Moab, he and his wife and his two sons. The name of the man was Elimelech and the name of his wife Naomi, and the names of his two sons were Mahlon and Chilion. They were Ephrathites from Bethlehem in Judah" (Ruth 1:1-2). This family lived about a century before the time of David when Israel was experiencing lawlessness, confusion, and unfaithfulness to God. There was a severe famine in Israel at that time. The famine was the determinative factor in the family's decision to move to Moab. Rather than rely on

God in Bethlehem, the family decided to move to a godless land for provision.

Moab

The Moabites were descendants of Lot's eldest daughter through her incestuous relationship with her own father (Genesis 19:29-35). "Thus the daughters of Lot became pregnant by their father. The firstborn bore a son and called his name Moab. He is the father of the Moabites to this day" (Genesis 19:36-37). Even though their relationships had close kinships, the Moabites and Israelites despised one another. The Moabites were a pagan nation who worshipped gods, primarily a god called Chemosh. Worship of this idol was grotesque and at times even involving human sacrifices. Moabite paganism was the epitome of idolatry and represented everything the Israelites were supposed to avoid. It is rather surprising that

Elimelech, a landowner and by all accounts prominent in Bethlehem, moved his family to this abominable place.

Naomi

Naomi's faith and character indicate that the family of Elimelech were devout Jews. The famine must have been extraordinarily severe for this family to move to such a spiritually desolate pagan land. "But Elimelech, the husband of Naomi died, and she was left with her two sons. These took Moabite wives; the name of the one Orpha and the name of the other Ruth. They lived about ten years, and both Mahlon and Chilion died, so that the woman was left without her two sons and her husband" (Ruth 1:3-4). Naomi found herself in a distant pagan land. As if things were not challenging enough, she lost her husband and both sons.

The marriages of Naomi's sons were not ideal as they married Moabite women. A Moabite was considered an illegitimate. Naomi obviously accepted these daughters-in-law into her family, loved them, and discipled them. Naomi's love for these women was obvious. The responsibility she assumed for them was admirable. Naomi lost everything. She left her home and all that was familiar to relocate to a pagan land. She lost her husband. She lost both sons, and was left as a widow to fend for herself and her widowed daughters-in-law. Nowhere do we read that Naomi gave up on God. Nowhere do we read that Naomi gave in to fear, unbelief, anger, or unforgiveness. In spite of her desperate circumstances, when all hope seemed lost, she remained devoted to Jehovah.

Obstacles to Spiritual Growth

Naomi surely faced a gamut of emotions. She had choices. She could have given into the crippling effects of fear and anxiety, but chose to trust in God. Women in the

Twenty-First Century still struggle with the debilitating effects of fear and anxiety.

"Fear is defined as a distressing emotion aroused by impending danger, evil, pain, etc., whether the threat is real or imagined" (Webster 2001, 291). Fear is a natural emotion and can take on a positive or negative connotation. "In the Hebrew language, fear refers to reverence, carefulness, concern, fright, dread or terror. Fear is that affection of the mind that arises with the awareness of approaching danger" (Unger 1985 [1957], 404). Fear can be both healthy and unhealthy. It becomes unhealthy when fear consumes us to the point that it takes the focus away from God, and we become so obsessed with its consequences that we lose perspective. Fear can entangle to the point of devastation. Healthy fear warns us to avoid or prepare for impending or potential danger. "Fear pertaining to God is of several kinds: superstitious, which is the fruit of ignorance; servile which leads to abstinence from many sins through apprehension of punishment; and filial, which has its spring in love and prompts to care not to offend God and to endeavor in all things to please him" (Unger 1985 [1957], 404). We would be wise to fear God in reverence and awe, to trust him in all circumstances, accept his sovereignty and allow his goodness and mercy to guide us through the impossible, improbable and unimaginable. "Since we have these promises, beloved, let us cleanse ourselves from every defilement of body and spirit, bringing holiness to completion in the fear of God" (2 Corinthians 7:1).

"Unbelief is incredulity or skepticism, especially in matters of religious faith" (Webster 2001, 852). "Believe in the Hebrew language means to remain steadfast, to be persuaded, to adhere to, and rely on" (Unger 1985 [1957], 154). The absence of belief is to falter, to question, to lose hold of, to waiver, to be indecisive and unsure. "In a scriptural sense faith in its larger usage represents four principle ideas: confidence in God, a creedal or doctrinal concept of the essential body of revealed truth, faithfulness as an evidence of fruit of the believer's trust in God, and a designation of Christ as the object of faith" (Unger 1985 [1957], 154). Unbelief is the quintessential demise of humanity.

Twenty-First Century Women

In today's culture, women are faced with two life altering questions. Do we believe that God is who he says he is? This first question deals with the fundamental principle of salvation. "If you confess with your mouth that Jesus is Lord and believe in your heart that God raised him from the dead, you will be saved" (Romans 10:9). The absence of knowing God, truly knowing him, leads to a life of hopelessness, despair, and utter failure. Salvation in and of itself assures life after death. Salvation assures the believer of eternal life. God desires more. He desires a relationship with his people. What are we willing to do, to give or to give up for a relationship with God? Are we willing to deny self, repent and submit to God?

Secondly, do we believe that God will do what he says he will do? This question involves trust. "Trust is a confident and sure reliance on the integrity, strength, ability, of a person or thing. Trust is a confident expectation of hope" (Webster 2001, 844). Trust can be used as a noun or verb. As a verb, it is in perfect and past perfect active tense. It can be used in a passive voice. "Trust has been translated in some forms to mean hope" (Vine 1996 [1984], 646). Trust involves relinquishing oneself to the authority of someone or something for gain. We can obviously place our trust in unworthy and unreliable objects. Trust in anything or anyone but God is circumstantial. Trusting in circumstances lends to pain, disappointment, and uncertainty.

We have to determine where we stand and in whom we trust. The ultimate benefit of salvation determines whether or not we are all in. "Trust in the Lord forever, for the Lord God is an everlasting rock" (Isaiah 26:4). God does not change. He does not desert or forsake. He does not waiver. God is reliable. God is certain. God is trustworthy. He has proven it.

"Anger is the emotion of distant displeasure and indignation arising from the feeling of injury done or intended, from a discovery of offense against the law. Anger is sinful when it arises too soon, without reflection; when the injury that awakens it is only apparent; when it is disproportionate to the offense; when it is transferred from the guilty to the innocent; when it is too long protracted and becomes vengeful" (Unger 1985 [1957], 62). Anger is a verb. It requires effort. It requires work. Anger is unproductive. "Know this, my beloved brothers: let every person be quick to hear, slow to speak, slow to anger; for the anger of man does not produce the righteousness of God" (James 1:19).

Unforgiveness is the inability or refusal to grant pardon for or remission of an offense that leads to resentment. Unforgiveness refers to the inability to dismiss or release. As a verb, it means to bestow a favor unconditionally. "In scripture forgiveness signifies the remission of the punishment due to sinful conduct, the deliverance of the sinner from the penalty divinely and therefore, righteously, imposed; it involves the complete removal of the cause of the offense; such remission is based upon the vicarious and propitiatory sacrifice of Christ" (Vine 1996 [1984], 250). Unforgiveness is a cancer among women in our society – including the church. Unforgiveness is destructive and accomplishes nothing positive or productive. The thought process involves punishing the one to whom forgiveness is withheld. The unfortunate truth is unforgiveness punishes the one withholding forgiveness. Unforgiveness destroys relationships, families, marriages, homes, institutions and churches. Unforgiveness stealthily and relentlessly eats away at the emotional, physical, and spiritual psyche. It is withheld to the detriment of the one who refused to forgive. We are commanded to forgive as Christ forgave us. There are no exclusions in forgiveness. There are no exceptions. It is to be complete. What someone else may or may not have done to offend is not the issue. It is a condition of the heart. What we do, how we act, our responses and reactions determine what we believe about God. "Put on then, as God's chosen ones, holy and beloved, compassionate hearts, kindness, humility, meekness and patience, bearing with one another and, if one has a complaint against another, forgiving each other, as the Lord has forgiven you, so you must forgive" (Colossians 3:13). Forgiveness is not a choice for believers.

The one commonality in these obstacles is sin. Sin separates us from God. Is that really a risk worth taking? If we intend to be women after God's own heart, if we hope to make an impact in this world, we must relinquish all rights to ourselves and honor God with our lives. That will require intentionally letting go of those things that hold us hostage. We must refuse to be victims of sin. Complete freedom is found in forgiveness.

The Daughters-in-Law

Husbandless and childless, Naomi found herself in a less than ideal situation. Old and weary, she longed to return to her homeland of Palestine. Hearing news that the famine had ended in Palestine, Naomi determined to return. Parting from loved ones is never easy. Under the circumstances, it would seem necessary for Naomi and her two daughters-in-law to part ways. Naomi pled with the women to return to their mother's houses. She had nothing to offer them. With much trepidation, Orpah returned to her mother's house. Ruth was emphatic. "Do not urge me to leave you or turn back from following you; for where you go, I will go, and where you lodge, I will lodge; your people shall be my people, and your God, my God. Where you die, I will die, and there I will be buried. Thus may the Lord do to me and worse, if anything but death parts you and me" (Ruth1:16-17). Ruth resolved to leave her family, friends, and homeland for a far away, unfamiliar land, and an uncertain future. Ruth's love for Naomi was unconditional, without reserve, and determined. Her commitment was steadfast and certain. This evidences Ruth's resolute conversion. Ruth had a saving faith that came from belief in God. "Behold, God is my salvation; I will trust and not be afraid; for the Lord God is my strength and my song, and he had become my salvation" (Isaiah 12:2). Ruth made a decision to place her faith and trust in the one true God. Ruth gave up everything that was familiar to follow and care for her aged mother-in-law. There is no record of complaint as Ruth served unselfishly enduring many trials that followed. Ruth's character revealed her true conversion. Ruth was a Gentile, a heathen girl, from a pagan land, a worshipper of idols.

Faith cannot occur without repentance. "Repentance is a heartfelt sorrow for sin, a renouncing of it, and a sincere commitment to forsake it and walk in obedience to Christ. It is importance to realize that sorrow or deep remorse for our actions does not constitute genuine repentance unless it is accompanied by a sincere decision to forsake sin that is being committed against God" (Grudem 2000, 713). We are left without doubt that Ruth was genuinely converted.

Ruth later married Boaz, a kinsman of Naomi's deceased husband. He was the son of Salmon, the husband of Rahab the harlot. Their union resulted in the royal bloodline of David and consequently Jesus the Messiah.

Ruth and Boaz were King David's great-grandparents. It is important to emphasize that Jesus' bloodline included two Gentile women, Rahab and Ruth.

A Note on Singleness

It is not fair to emphasize roles of women as primarily wives and mothers. "There were one hundred two million single people ages eighteen and older in America in 2011. That is forty-four point one percent of the entire population in America" (U.S. Census 2012). Many single contemporary men and women have served faithfully, productively, and profitably. "Then Peter answered and said to Jesus, 'Behold, we have left everything and followed you; what then will there be for us…And everyone who has left houses or brothers or sisters, or father or mother or children or farms for My names sake, shall receive many times as much, and shall inherit eternal life'"(Matthew 19:27, 29). Christians know that Christ will more than compensate for every cost incurred by being single and serving Christ. "Marriage as we know it in this age is not the final destiny of any human" (Piper & Grudem 2006, 18). The social, emotional, and physical costs of singleness will be outweighed by socializing with Jesus around his throne, involvement with families who desperately need to know Christ, and in producing spiritual children.

"But I want you to be free from concern. One who is unmarried is concerned about the things of the Lord, how he may please the Lord; but one who is married is concerned about the things of the world, and how he may please his wife, and his interests are divided" (1 Corinthians 7:32-34a). The Apostle Paul was not married and enjoyed freedom for ministry. The single lifestyle enables one to get the most out of the time God allows for his work. Flexibility, time constraints, and schedules are less challenging. One of the greatest sacrifices of singles is their loneliness. It takes great courage to be single. "Singleness has been a noble and courageous path for ministry ever since Jesus and the Apostle Paul chose it because of the kingdom of heaven. The courage comes when you sense God calling you to singleness and you accept the call with zeal and creative planning for his glory" (Piper & Grudem 2006, 23).

"Yet I wish that all men were as I, myself, am. However each man has his own gift from God, one in this manner and another in that. But I say to the unmarried and widows that it is good for them if they remain even as I" (1 Corinthians 7:7-8). The Apostle Paul calls singleness a gift. Genesis 2:18 says, "It is not good for man to be alone." This verse indicates that singleness is not good. How do we reconcile this? If it is not good, how can it be a gift from God? The answer is Genesis 2:18 occurred before the fall. Sometimes it is good to be alone. Almost no one has to be alone. God created us to have relationships.

There is plenty of opportunity for that in ministry. We must trust in God's sovereignty. God is sufficient in all circumstances. Jesus Christ is Lord of our lives, and we must trust his wisdom.

Whether single or married, our womanhood matters. Our maturity in Christ is not dependent upon our marital status. "Our prayer is that God will give Christian singles a deep understanding and appreciation for their own distinct sexual personhood, that Christ will be magnified more and more in you as you offer your gift of singleness back to him in radical freedom from the way of the world, and that you will grow deeper and deeper in joyful devotion to the triumphant cause of Christ" (Piper & Grudem 2006, 28).

"I tell you the truth, you will weep and mourn while the world rejoices. You will grieve, but your grief will turn to joy." (John 16:20)

Chapter Six

A Woman and a King

"Bathsheba was the daughter of Ammiel (1 Chronicles 3:5). Ammiel was the son of Gemalli, of the tribe of Dan, one of the twelve spies sent by Moses to explore the land of Canaan" (Unger 1985 [1957], 52). Bathsheba was a member of one of the twelve tribes of Israel. "Bathsheba was the wife of Uriah, one of David's faithful generals who was fighting the Ammonitish war (II Samuel 11:3-13). "She was beautiful in appearance" (2 Samuel 11:2b).

David was a shepherd, a warrior, musician, outlaw, faithful friend, empire builder, sinner, saint, failed father and exemplary King. "About 1000 B.C. David was installed as King over all Israel. David took a weak, dispirited nation and made it an empire and expanded the kingdom's border. David captured Jerusalem and established the city as the royal and religious capital of Israel, a dynasty that lasted nearly half a millennium" (Gardner 1994, 78-79). It was during David's reign as King and during the war against Ammon that Bathsheba's story begins.

Bathsheba

Bathsheba's husband, Uriah was serving in King David's army during a siege of the Ammonite capital. Bathsheba's home was in view of King David's new palace in Jerusalem. "It happened late one afternoon, when David arose from his couch and was walking on the roof of the king's house that he saw from the roof a woman bathing, and the woman was very beautiful" (II Samuel 11:2). Bathsheba was bathing in the courtyard of her home, in the evening, apparently when others had gone to bed. "Oriental homes had an enclosed courtyard that was considered part of the house. Bathsheba, bathing herself by lamplight was not immodest as she was in her house. However, the interior of the courtyard could be seen from the roof of David's house" (ESV 2011, 366). Problem number one, David saw a beautiful woman bathing and his eyes lingered. "Bathsheba was going through the monthly purification ritual following menstruation" (Alexander 2009, 270). "In the case of menstruation, the period of impurity was for seven days. Anyone who touched her would be unclean until evening. Anything she touched, sat on or laid on would be rendered unclean" (Leviticus 15:16-24). The purification process was lengthy and arduous, and the ritual would have been obvious. This information reveals that Bathsheba definitely was not pregnant before she was brought to David.

This lingering of David's eyes was deliberate, leading to great temptation that culminated in sin. It is important to note David's position of power as King. "David was not only commander in chief of the army and supreme judge, but he had absolute master of the lives of his subjects" (Unger 1985 [1957], 739).

Problem number two, "David sent and inquired about the woman" (II Samuel 11:3a). Even after David was told who she was, the wife of Uriah, one of David's special guards in battle, he sent for her. We have no information regarding Bathsheba's position or early involvement in the commencement of these circumstances. She likely did not know why she had been summoned by the king. According to the laws, Bathsheba could not have resisted had she desired, for a woman in ancient times was completely subject to a king's will…If he desired her, he could have her" (Deen 1983, 114). Problem number three, "David sent messengers and took her, and when she came to him, he lay with her; and when she had purified herself from her uncleanness, she returned to her house"

(II Samuel 11:4). Uncleanness in this context refers to the emission of bodily fluids resulting from an intimate act. "Purification was effected by bathing the body and washing in running water" (Unger 1985 [1957], 1317). Obviously Bathsheba bathed at the Palace before returning home (Leviticus 15:18). This raises a question. Why did Bathsheba bathe at the palace rather than return to her home to bathe? Does this indicate complicity on her part? David had no desire to marry Bathsheba. He pridefully and selfishly wanted her temporarily for his pleasure.

Bathsheba could have been consensual in this act. Maybe she feared reprisal toward her husband had she refused David's advances. David was the highest authority in the land and extremely handsome. As the wife of a soldier on the battlefield, Bathsheba would have been alone for quite some time. She may have been complicit in the tryst or she may have been a victim. Regardless of Bathsheba's responsibility, whether or not the act was consensual, sin's consequences directly affected her. Bathsheba found herself with child. By this time, she was probably a few months pregnant. The sense of timing would have been urgent. Bathsheba's pregnancy in the absence of her husband would suggest adultery. The punishment for adultery was death by stoning. In an effort to protect both he and Bathsheba, David plotted a cover-up. David ordered Uriah to return to Jerusalem under the premise of reporting to him on the war. David's plan was to have Uriah return from battle to sleep with Bathsheba to cover up his sin of adultery. Uriah refused to see his wife or sleep with her because of his loyalty to his comrades in battle. David then ordered him to the front lines of battle to ensure he would be killed. David devised a plan for the murder of Uriah in an effort cover up his illicit affair with Bathsheba. With Uriah out of the way, there would be no accuser. There is no information concerning how much Bathsheba knew of David's involvement in the murder of her husband. Regardless, she would have been compelled to avoid any public scrutiny concerning her condition.

"When the wife of Uriah heard that Uriah her husband was dead, she lamented over him" (II Samuel 11:26). When the seven day period of mourning for Uriah passed, David had Bathsheba brought to the palace and made her his wife. The child was born. "And the Lord afflicted the child that Uriah's wife bore to David, and he became sick" (II Samuel 12:15b). It is at this point that desperation is all consuming and God's favor is coveted. David, the man of God, had fallen from grace. The consequences of his sin were inconceivable. The sin was David's and perhaps Bathsheba's as well. Regardless, the penalty for sin was borne by both David and Bathsheba. They both endured the incredible pain of losing a child. How do we reconcile God's love and compassion when faced with the unthinkable? We expect to lose those aged people we love, although at times the loss is untimely and most difficult to endure. However, the loss of a child is incomprehensible. Amid the throes of suffering and grief, we can trust that God, in his sovereignty, does not waste pain and suffering. He uses everything in creation to accomplish his purposes.

Sovereignty

Sovereignty is God's exercise of power over his creation. "By ascribing to God's absolute power, it is not meant that God is not free from all the restraints of reason and morality, but he is able to do everything that is in harmony with his wise, holy, and perfect nature" (Unger 1985 [1957], 942). As the all-powerful Creator, God preserves and governs everything in the universe. How does God's sovereignty and goodness measure up when life sinks to such depths as with the loss of a child? How could such anguish be a part of God's plan? "God is the central figure behind even the tragic events in our lives. He is in ultimate and complete control. Not even the enemy can touch us without God's permission, and even then God overrules and works through Satan's schemes to accomplish good for us" (Custis James 2001, 87).

Though the word providence is not found in Scripture, it is used to summarize God's ongoing relationship with his creation. "God's providence may be defined as follows: God is continually involved with all created things in such a way that he (1) keeps them existing and maintaining the properties with which he created them (2) cooperates with created things in every action, directing their distinctive properties to cause them to act as they do (3) directs them to fulfill his purposes" (Grudem 1999, 142). In preservation, God continues to give us the breath we breathe. Molecules, cells, air, weather, vegetation, water, the solar system and all of creation continue to act as they were created to act. God sustains the universe. In concurrence, God causes all things to happen and he does so in such a way that he upholds our ability to make willing, responsible choices that have real and eternal results, and for which we are held accountable. Acts 4:24-30 is a prayer of thanksgiving for the sovereign power of God "to do whatever your (God's) hand and your (God's) plan had predestined to take place." God spares no joy or pain, loss or gain, in getting us to that place where we get it, where we finally, once and for all, acknowledge our need for him. It is here, it is the moment of acute awareness, that we understand our personal nothingness and hopelessness. It is here where we acknowledge our individual incompetence, failures and insufficiencies, our spiritual bankruptcy. It is in this nanosecond that our desperation for God becomes all consuming. David and Bathsheba found themselves in the throes of suffering for their sin.

Repentance

In the case of evil, God never does evil and can never be blamed for it. "The blame for evil is always on the responsible creature, whether man or demon, who does it, and the creature who does it is always worthy of punishment" (Grudem 1994, 329). Where does free will fit into all of this? Considering God's course in fulfilling his purposes, we have the freedom to make choices, but we are not free to make decisions outside God's control and power. God works though human actions, even though God holds us responsible for wrong actions. Sin has real and eternal results. Where does personal responsibility for our actions lead?

Answering that question requires repentance. "Repentance is a heartfelt sorrow for sin, a renouncing of it, and a sincere commitment to forsake it and walk in obedience to Christ. Repentance, like faith, is an intellectual understanding (that sin is wrong), an emotional approval of the teachings of Scripture regarding sin (a sorrow for sin and hatred for it), and a personal decision to turn from sin (a renouncing of sin and a decision of the will to forsake it and lead a life of obedience to Christ instead)" (Gruden 1994, 310). Genuine saving faith must be accompanied by repentance for sin. Genuine repentance is evidenced in a changed life. It is an attitude of the heart. How we act, how we live reflects what we believe about God. Repentance of sin is a humble act of submission and intentional obedience to Christ. The ultimate consummation of recognizing sin and genuine repentance for sin is a saving faith in Jesus Christ. In redemption, we are saved, delivered, liberated from our sin and guilt. Jesus Christ is the one and only means by which we are saved. Redemption was purchased by the shed blood of Christ by his death on the cross, his resurrection, and ascension to heaven where he is seated at the right hand of God.

The End of the Story

"Uriah is dead. The wedding is over; the child is born and becomes sick. The affair with Bathsheba, the murder of Uriah all seemed to have blown over" (Alexander 2009, 272). "And the Lord sent Nathan to David" (II Samuel 12:1a). Nathan was a prophet who used a parable to lead David to condemn his own actions and bring about repentance. David's confession was immediate as was God's gracious forgiveness (II Samuel 12:13). David's confession is found in Psalm 51, God's forgiveness in Psalm 32. We know that David was used exceedingly of God. "This is not the end of the relationship with Bathsheba, nor is she rejected: for out of the grief and the comforting comes another form of life, and the Lord loved the boy (Solomon)" (Alexander, 2009, 272). "Then David comforted his wife, Bathsheba, and went in to lay with her, and she bore a son, and he called his name Solomon"

(II Solomon 12:24). Solomon became king after his father, David. In addition to Solomon, Bathsheba bore three other sons with David. She either became the favored wife of David or David's life with her was an appeasement. David's life with her likely resulted from his repentance and desire to please God. When King David was nearing the end of his life, Bathsheba carried out the most important mission of her life. She intervened to have her son Solomon succeed his father as king of Israel. "Only an intelligent, respected woman, in whom the aged king had great confidence, could have won such a victory. Only a righteous woman, it would seem, could have been sought out by the prophet Nathan" (Deen 1955, 116). The prophet Nathan who had once denounced David, conspired with Bathsheba to have Solomon made king is evidence that she had won great respect. "Solomon obviously loved and respected his mother as he gave her a place of honor as queen mother on his right side, a place of honor and authority" (Deen 1955, 116). Not only is Bathsheba mentioned in 1 Chronicles 3:5 as the mother of David's four sons, but she is listed in the genealogy of Jesus in Matthew 1:6.

Sanctification

Sanctification is the purification of the believer. This sanctification must be learned from God; it is God's will for the believer and his purpose in calling believers by the Holy Spirit to salvation (1Thessalonians 4:3-7). God teaches sanctification by his word (John 17:17). Sanctification must be pursued by the believer, earnestly, devotedly and faithfully (Romans 12:1, Hebrews 12:14). "For the holy character is not vicarious, it cannot be transferred or imputed, it is an individual possession, built up, little by little, as a result of obedience to the Word of God, and of following the example of Christ in the power of the Holy Spirit" (Vine 1996 [1984], 545-546).

David's was Israel's most famous king. His life was filled with trials, tribulations, struggles, pain, depression, sorrow, grief, devastation and desperation. David's sin was great, and his acknowledgment of his sin evidenced. His repentance was sincere. David experienced God's complete forgiveness. David is referred to as the man after God's own heart, and his relentless pursuit of God appears in God's Word. David is the author of seventy-three of the one hundred fifty Psalms in the Old Testament. Bathsheba, like David had a tumultuous life. Like David, it is evident that she ended well.

Overcoming Twenty-First Century Challenges

Bathsheba's story offers its readers eternal help, hope and salvation. All of us can relate in some way to the gamut of emotions she experienced. There is certainly nothing we women of the Twenty-First Century will experience that Bathsheba did not. Consider the guilt and shame, the regrets and what ifs. We women are our own worst enemies. We are much too hard on ourselves. We tend to dwell on the bad stuff. We listen to the lies and buy into them, perhaps because the bad stuff is easier to believe. This focus on self is dishonoring to God. Christ died for our sin and guilt. His forgiveness was complete. His sacrifice was enough to wholly cover our sin. His forgiveness is certain. We need to fully place our trust in God, relinquish all rights to ourselves, and seek him with all our hearts. We must seek to become holy as he is holy. Salvation is a gift that cannot be earned. We are conditional beings. God's love and forgiveness is not conditional on who or what we are. His love and forgiveness is based on Christ, his death, and resurrection. Once we accept Christ as our Savior, we become children, daughters of God! "He saved us, not because of works done by us in righteousness, but according to his own mercy, by the washing of regeneration and renewal of the Holy Spirit, whom he poured out on us richly through Jesus Christ our Savior, so that being justified by his grace we might become heirs according to the hope of eternal life" (Titus 3:5-7). It is time we live like it.

> *"The time has come. The kingdom of God is near. Repent and believe the good news!"*
> *(Mark 1:15)*

Chapter 7

Mary, Mother of God

Very little is said about the ancestry of Mary. "She was a relative of Elizabeth (Luke 1:36), the mother of John the Baptist, who was of the tribe of Levi. John 19:25 mentions a sister and in comparison with Mark 15:40 and Matthew 27:56, it is almost certain that this was Salome, wife of Zebedee, in which case James and John were cousins of Jesus" (Tenney 1976 [1975], 107). "The references to the house of David by Elizabeth and Zechariah (Luke 1:32, 69), and the frequent, unchallenged, public address of Jesus by the title "Son of David" (Matthew 9:27, 15:22, 20:30, 31, Mark 10:47, 48) imply that on His mother's side as well as Joseph's, Jesus was from David's line" (Tenney 1976 [1975], 106-107). "Mary's branch of David's family tree can be traced through David's son Nathan, while Joseph's branch is royal line, through Solomon. Therefore, Christ inherited David's throne through his stepfather, as was his birthright as a firstborn son" (MacArthur 2005, 110).

Mary was brought up in Nazareth, a city in Galilee. Nazareth was an insignificant town of low regard. "The disrepute in which Nazareth stood (John 1:46) has generally been attributed to the Galilean's lack of culture and rude dialect. It would seem probable in an ethical sense that the people of Nazareth had a bad name among their neighbors for irreligion or some laxity of morals" (Unger 1985 [1957], 907-908). Mary was an obscure peasant girl. Her life would not have been without hardships. She was probably still in her teens when she was betrothed to Joseph. "Her arranged betrothal was a legal engagement known as kiddushin, which in that culture typically lasted a full year. Kiddushin was as legally binding as marriage itself and only legal divorce could dissolve the marriage contract" (MacArthur 2005, 112). If the betrothed man died before consummation of the marriage, the woman became a widow, and the custom of levirate marriage might apply to her. Only through a writing of divorce could she be dismissed from the betrothal relationship. Any sexual relationship during the betrothal period was treated as adultery, which resulted in divorce.

"During the period of betrothal the angel Gabriel visited Mary and greeted her. Mary was puzzled by the greeting, and evidently frightened, for the angel continued, telling her not to be afraid, and that she would conceive and bear a son whom she would call Jesus" (Tenney 1976, [1975], 107). "And Mary said to the angel, 'How can this be since I am a virgin?' And the angel answered her, 'The Holy Spirit will come upon you, and the power of the Most High will overshadow you; therefore the child to be born will be called holy-the Son of God'" (Luke 1:34-35). God's choice of Mary for the mother of Christ indicates her extraordinary faith and obedience to him. By all accounts, Mary was a nobody living in a nothing community. She had no credentials, no claim to fame. She led the life of a struggling peasant. "It is clear that Mary's young heart and mind were already thoroughly saturated with the Word of God…Her worship was clearly from the heart. She was plainly consumed by the wonder of God's grace to her (MacArthur 2005 116, 119). She stood out above all others as the most blessed and highly favored by God.

"And Mary said, 'Behold, I am the servant of the Lord; let it be to me according to your word. And the angel departed from her'" (Luke 1:38). It was the humble acceptance of the embarrassment, suspicion and misunderstanding that would undoubtedly follow, by this lowly, devout maiden (Tenney 1976, [1975], 109). Though faced with serious problems concerning her impending marriage and the social implications of her pregnancy, nowhere is there a reference of her unwillingness to submit completely to the will of the Father. She accepted this announcement with faith and resignation. Mary no doubt experienced fear, trepidation, and uncertainty. "Now the birth of Jesus Christ took place this way. When his mother Mary had been betrothed to Joseph, before they came together she was found to be with child from the Holy Spirit. And her husband, Joseph, being a just man and unwilling to put her to shame, resolved to divorce her quietly" (Matthew 1:18-19). Joseph determined to divorce Mary secretly rather than expose her assumed infidelity. He determined to avoid yielding Mary up to the law to suffer the penalty for adultery. "But as he considered these things, behold, an angel of the Lord appeared to him in a dream, saying, 'Joseph, son of David do not fear to take Mary as your wife, for that which is conceived in her is from the Holy Spirit. She will bear a son and you shall call his name Jesus, for he will save his people from their sins'" (Matthew 1:20-21). God performed an intervention, and

Joseph became the earthly stepfather of Jesus Christ. He no doubt had questions, concerns, and fears. However, Joseph submitted in obedience to the Father's will.

"There is no evidence that Mary ever brooded over the affects her pregnancy would have on her reputation. She instantly, humbly and joyfully submitted to God's will without further doubt or question. She could barely have a more godly response to the announcement of Jesus' birth" (MacArthur 2005, 114). Mary was a woman of remarkable faith and a true worshipper of God. Her joy over God's plan for her life was clearly evident. "Mary's life was significant for at least three reasons: She was a firsthand witness of Jesus' divine origin and true humanity. She was a tremendous model of godliness, faith, dedication, and patience, among other good qualities. She, along with other women, was incorporated into the new life of the church at Pentecost" (Piper & Grudem 2006, 119). Mary conceived, carried and delivered the Christ. She bore the one who came to reconcile man to God through his life, death, burial and resurrection. She bore witness to the entire life of Christ. She was there when he came into the world, and she watched as he suffered the vilest, most cruel death imaginable on a cross. She bore witness to the greatest of all events, the resurrection of her son from the dead to ascend into heaven to take his place at the right hand of the Father. Mary is the single, greatest witness to the life of Christ. The son she bore died, defeated death, and was resurrected to save all of humanity from their sins. She was there when his church began. Mary completely submitted to God's plan for her life, and she submitted to Christ, her son and her Savior. She was truly blessed among women.

    Mary lived with her husband, Joseph, in Nazareth after the birth of Christ. It is thought that Joseph died before Jesus entered his public ministry due to no mention of him in later gospel stories following the pilgrimage to Jerusalem for the Passover when Jesus was twelve years old. Mary and Joseph had at least six other children after the birth of Jesus. "Is not this the carpenter, the son of Mary and brother of James and Joses and Judas and Simon? Are not his sisters here with us" (Mark 6:3)? Four brothers are named, and sisters are plural, indicating at least two sisters. Scripture reveals that his brothers likely did not believe that Jesus was the Messiah until he appeared to James after the resurrection. "Then he appeared to James, then all the apostles" (1 Corinthians 15:7). This could provide explanation of why Jesus, when on the cross, committed his mother to John's care. "When Jesus saw his mother and the disciple whom he loved standing nearby, he said to his mother, 'Woman, behold your son.' Then he said to the disciple, 'Behold, your mother.' And from that hour the disciple took her to his own home" (John 19:26-27). Perhaps Jesus committed Mary to her nephew, John, rather than her other sons because John was single and his brothers were married. "Do we not have the right to take along a believing wife, as do the other apostles and the brothers of the Lord and Cephas" (1 Corinthians 9:5)? This is further evidence that the Lord's brothers were married, supporting reason for Jesus declaration to Mary and to John. "Perhaps Jesus intended for John to take Mary from the harrowing scenes of the crucifixion, as he did so from the hour. Traditions say that Mary lived the rest of her life with John, either in Jerusalem or accompanying him to Ephesus" (Tenney 1976 [1975], 110). In his sovereignty, Christ made provision for his mother. In his darkest hour, Christ's love and devotion for his mother is evident. After the resurrection, Mary and Jesus' brothers were in Jerusalem with the eleven disciples in the upper room. They joined the disciples and the other women in prayer as they awaited the promise, the gift of the Holy Spirit. "All these with one accord were devoting themselves in prayer, together with the women, and Mary the mother of Jesus, and his brothers" (Acts 1:14). This is the last mention of Mary in the Scriptures.

"Mary was a humble village maiden who typifies all that is finest and noblest in Jewish womanhood" (Tenney 1976 [1975] 110). Her integrity, character, deep spiritual sensitivity, and complete obedience to God are evident. "Her training of her son as a child, her unwavering confidence in him, and her complete loyalty to him, even though there were times she did not fully understand him, all prepared her for the position she took among the earliest disciples in acknowledging him as Lord and Christ" (Tenney 1976 [1975], 111). "Let all the House of Israel therefore know for certain that God has made him both Lord and Christ, this Jesus whom you crucified" (Acts 2:36).

"While acknowledging that Mary was the most extraordinary of women, it is appropriate to inject a word of caution against the common tendency to elevate her too much. She was, after all, a woman - not a demigoddess of a quasi-deiform creature who somehow transcended the rest of her race" (MacArthur 2005, 107). We must be careful not to give glory or honor to anyone other than Christ and the Father. No person in the history of humanity has ever accomplished anything to be compared to Christ. Many have done great things and offered great acts of service to humanity. Never has anyone been killed, buried and resurrected as Savior of the world. No one can claim status as the Son of God, and no one has inspired documented history to support such claims. No one has stood the test of time spanning more than two thousand years and continued to maintain his identity and superiority. "Mary's Immaculate Conception and her supposed sinlessness is likewise without any scriptural foundation whatsoever" (MacArthur 2005, 109-110). "The unique high privilege bestowed on this specially chosen maiden in no way suggests that worship should be offered to her" (Tenney

1976 [1975], 111). Worship belongs to God alone. Nothing in God's Word offers any indication otherwise. Mary was an ordinary girl chosen by God to be the mother of the Christ. God, in his sovereign will determined the means, the mode, the time and place to enter the world. God became flesh. "And Jesus answered him, 'It is written, you shall worship the Lord your God and him only shall you serve'" (Luke 4:8). Mary was the mother of Christ, an ordinary flesh and blood woman. She was a daughter of Eve, created in God's image and through Adam she inherited a sin nature, as did all of humanity. Jesus is fully God and fully man. Like his mother, Jesus had a human body and mind, a human soul, and human emotions. He was different in one respect: He was without sin. The virgin birth was the means God used to send his Son into a hostile world to save the people of the world from themselves. "To complete the Biblical teaching about Jesus Christ, we must affirm not only that he was fully human, but that he was fully divine" (Grudem 1999, 236). Jesus is God. God incarnate entered the world through a human vessel, to be a substitute sacrifice for all mankind. "Jesus' human body was like ours in every respect before his resurrection, and after his resurrection it was still a human body with 'flesh and bones,' but made perfect, the kind of body that we will have when Christ returns and we are raised from the dead as well" (Grudem 1999, 231).

Women in the Twenty-First Century Church

Mary, the mother is Jesus is an exemplary example for women in the church today. Her humility, profound spirituality, obedience, complete trust and submission are unrivaled. This woman experienced more pain, sorrow, grief and sheer joy than any woman who has ever lived. At a very young age, she was found with child and without husband. She became widowed when her children were young and faced raising her five boys and at least two girls alone. She watched as her first born son experienced ridicule and hate by his own people. She looked on as he was arrested and falsely accused. She stood by helplessly as her son was sentenced to death. She was there when Jesus was beaten beyond the recognition of a human being. She followed him as he struggled to carry his crucifixion cross up the hill to Golgotha where he would be killed by way of the cruelest and vilest death ever suffered. The pain this woman experienced was extraordinary. God the Father looked upon her with favor and spared her the final moments of her son's life, when Jesus breathed his last. Confused, dazed, and in shock from the horror of it all, John took her away at Jesus' request to spare her any further anguish. This extraordinary woman remained faithful and loyal through the greatest pain any mother can imagine. Her faith and loyalty are a source of hope for women today who feel alone in their pain, suffering, and grief. Her life is evidence that God never abandons his children. Her incomparable joy exceeded all pain, sorrow, and grief the moment she grasped the understanding of her son's accomplished mission. Her son became her Savior. She was there to hear the announcement of her Son's resurrection from the dead. She was there when the Holy Spirit descended at Pentecost. Mary, the mother of God, delivered him who was to become her Savior. Twenty-one centuries later, nothing has changed. "Jesus said, 'I am the way, and the truth, and the life. No one comes to the Father except through me'" (John 14:6). Mary the mother of Jesus found forgiveness for sin and salvation through repentance and faith in her Son. Nothing less and nothing more is required for anyone.

    God's will is for all people to know him, to have a relationship with him, and to be sanctified by the blood of Jesus. It is through the pain, sorrow, and anguish of life that we realize our deep need for Christ. God will allow whatever path necessary to get man/woman to the place where realization becomes reality. It is in suffering that we seek him. It is in pain that we call out to him. It is in our darkest hours that hope springs eternal. It was in the darkest hour of record that Christ willingly gave his life for all sin assuring his followers hope, peace, joy and life everlasting. His mother witnessed both the greatest loss and even greater gain. "For I know the plans I have for you, declares the Lord, plans for welfare and not for evil, to give you a future and a hope" (Jeremiah 29:11). Mary is the star witness to the personified and resurrected Christ. Her message to women today is, "Believe in the Lord Jesus Christ and be saved" (Acts 16:31).

"Trust in the Lord with all your heart and lean not on your own understanding; in all your ways acknowledge him, and he will make your paths straight." (Proverbs 3:5-6)

Chapter Eight

A Woman after God's Own Heart

Although there is little information about Mary of Bethany, she was an extraordinary friend and devoted follower of Jesus. Mary lived with her brother Lazarus and sister Martha in the small village of Bethany. "Bethany was within easy walking distance of Jerusalem, about two miles southeast of the temple's gate, just over the Mount of Olives from Jerusalem's city center" (MacArthur 2005, 155). Scriptures imply that Mary was younger than her sister, Martha. There is no mention of Mary ever having been married. "Now Jesus loved Martha and her sister and Lazarus" (John 11:5). Jesus seems to have been entertained frequently in their home. Mary's genuine love for and devotion to Jesus is evidenced in the Scriptures. The information provided about Mary involves three significant events.

Reception at Bethany

"Now as they went on their way, Jesus entered a village. And a woman named Martha welcomed him into her house. And she had a sister called Mary who sat at the Lord's feet and listened to his teaching" (Luke 10:38-39). The assumption is that Martha was the owner of the house. She was consumed with preparing and serving the meal. "Entertaining others to eat and stay was important for the people of the Bible…In New Testament times, refusal to give hospitality amounted to rejection and it was therefore essential for Christians to give hospitality" (Gower 2005, 214-215). Rather than being consumed with meal preparations, Mary sat at the feet of Jesus soaking in his every word. She was entirely consumed with Christ and oblivious to anything else. Mary was more concerned about Jesus' teaching than with meal preparation and service. Her actions did not indicate laziness or a lack of concern for their guests. The guest of honor was her all-consuming focus. Mary's failure to aid Martha in the preparations caused Martha to condemn her for abandoning the work that she deemed needed to be done. Martha should have commended Mary for her devotion to Christ rather than discourage her. "Christ justified Mary's choice, for she chose to be with Christ, and took a better way of honoring him and of pleasing him, by receiving his word into her heart" (Henry 1960, 1450). The Lord desires our affection above our service. While service to the Lord is the fruit of the Christian's life, service can be contaminated with pride and desire for the approval of others. Service before devotion reveals a deficient relationship with Jesus. Mary's undivided attention to Christ revealed a deeper understanding of him than most. She chose worshipping over all else.

The Death of Lazarus

Lazarus was the brother of Mary and Martha, probably the youngest of the three siblings. John 11:1-46 gives the account of the death of Lazarus. "Now a certain man was ill, Lazarus of Bethany, the village of Mary and Martha…So the sisters sent to him (Jesus) saying, 'Lord, he whom you love is ill'" (John 11:1, 3). Lazarus was a devoted and loved disciple who also enjoyed a special relationship with Christ. Mary and Martha knew Jesus was nearby and sent word to him concerning their brother's illness. "But when Jesus heard it he said, 'This illness does not lead to death. It is for the glory of God, so that the Son of God may be glorified through it'" (John 11:4). Christ would use the death of Lazarus to perform his greatest miracle, one that would signify his resurrection. Mary and Martha wanted Christ to know of Lazarus' sickness and believed he would come and help. It must have been confusing, disappointing, and discouraging to them when Jesus failed to immediately respond to their message. The religious climate in Judea had become hostile toward Jesus, putting him and his disciples at risk. The disciples were in no way inclined to return there as the Jews were seeking to harm Jesus. Jesus delayed his coming, and Lazarus died. Mary was deeply affected. After the fact, disregarding the risk, Jesus determined to return to Judea. "Now when Jesus came, he found Lazarus had already been in the tomb for four days" (John 11:17). When the sisters heard that Jesus was in route, Martha went to meet him but Mary stayed home. Jesus sent for Mary and she quickly responded. Mary rose quickly and went out, followed by the Jews who were mourning with her. "Now Mary came to where Jesus was and saw him, she fell at his feet, saying to him, 'Lord if you had been here, my brother would not have died'" (John 11:32). "Those that in a day of peace place themselves at Christ's feet, to receive instruction from him, may with comfort and confidence in a day of trouble cast themselves at his feet with hope to find favor with him" (Henry 1960, 1571). This act was Mary's confession of faith. She believed that Christ could have saved her brother had he arrived before Lazarus died. She did not yet understand that Christ would raise her brother from the dead. She understood and believed that Jesus was the Messiah; however, she did not yet understand God's redemption plan by way of the cross. Mary's profession of faith was in the presence of the Jews that attended her, both friends and family members. When Jesus saw the deep grief of Mary he was deeply moved. "The two sisters became the first women recorded in the New Testament to witness Jesus' expression of grief for a friend" (Deen 1983, 178). Their pain, sorrow, and grief drew them to Jesus. Their love and devotion to him did not waiver in their time of suffering. They expressed no anger in Jesus' failure to come to them when they sent for him. This was a great contrast to the jealousy and hate of Jesus' fierce opposition in Jerusalem. Friends and family members who accompanied Mary witnessed her confession of faith. Yet many of them were included among those who were enemies of Christ.

Jesus inquired as to where Lazarus was buried. The grave of Lazarus' burial was a cave with a stone laid upon it. Jesus ordered the stone to be removed. He prayed to the Father in the presence of the onlookers and called Lazarus out of the grave. Lazarus having been dead four days came forth. This is another significant event indicating what was to come in Jesus' near future. Some of those who witnessed this event believed. Others became more even hostile toward him. Mary seemed to sense the express danger Jesus had put himself in by giving life to her brother. Her gratitude and honor is shown in the final event involving her family. Jesus' arrest, trial, and death were on the horizon.

The Anointing of Jesus

Six days before the Passover, Jesus came to Bethany where he lodged with his friends Mary, Martha, and Lazarus who gave a dinner for him there. This feast would be his last in Bethany. "Mary therefore took a pound of expensive ointment made from pure nard, and anointed the feet of Jesus and wiped his feet with her hair. The house was filled with the fragrance of the perfume" (John 12:3). "This alabaster cruse of precious imported perfume from India represented a year's wages" Tenney 1976 [1975], 104). Mary's anointing of Christ disclosed an acute perspective of knowledge and understanding of the person and deity of Christ. This act of honor, worship, and adoration was exceptional. This was the greatest tribute Mary could have made to him. In this act, she revealed her unequivocal devotion to him. Her service and devotion was a believing love expressed by faith in Jesus as the Messiah. Jesus considered Mary's anointing a most appropriate and beautiful tribute. "In pouring this ointment on my body, she has done it to prepare me for burial. Truly, I say to you, whenever this gospel is proclaimed in the whole world, what she has done will also be told in memory of her" (Matthew 26:12-13). Mary, in some sense, understood that she was anointing Jesus for burial. She knew that her brother's resurrection would solidify Jesus' enemy's resolve to put him to death. "Mary seemed to be able to discern Jesus' true meaning even better than any of the twelve disciples. Her gesture of anointing him in preparation for his burial at the beginning of that final week in Jerusalem shows a remarkably mature understanding" (MacArthur 2005, 165). This was no routine anointment. Mary of Bethany had her priorities in order. Jesus knew she loved and adored him. He knew she believed in him. Her worship of him was evidence of her service to him. Jesus did not show partiality between genders. He looked at the heart. It is of great importance to know that in Jesus' day, women were not taught by rabbis. Jesus cut across cultural barriers to elevate women to a position of equality. Women ministered with and to Jesus during his ministry on earth. The women stuck with him. Women were those he stopped to comfort on the road to Golgotha. To the mourning and lamenting women, Jesus said, "Daughters of Jerusalem, do not weep for me, but weep for yourselves and your children" (Luke 23:28). When Jesus, on the cross, breathed his last, the Centurion declared Christ's innocence. All the crowds that had assembled to watch left in anguish and grief. "And all the acquaintances and the women who had followed him from Galilee stood at a distance watching these things" (Luke 23:49). When Jesus looked down from the cross, he saw the women. Many of the men had scattered in fear. When Jesus was taken for burial, the women were there. "The women who had come with him from Galilee followed and saw the tomb and how his body was laid" (Luke 23:55). It was the women who first returned to the tomb with prepared spices and ointments. When they arrived, the stone was rolled away, and the body of Jesus was gone. It was a woman to whom Jesus first appeared after he rose from the grave. Mary Magdalene stood weeping outside the empty tomb, devastated that his body was gone (assuming it had been stolen) and became the first to witness the risen Christ. In fact, she had a conversation with him. She became the first evangelist. Of all the men Jesus could have first revealed himself – his beloved disciples, his brothers, Lazarus – he appeared to a woman. A note on Lazarus: several men and women who died were returned to life as recorded in both the Old Testament and the New Testament. These people did, however, die at a later date. Christ is the only one who has ever been resurrected from death never to experience death again. He lives. He was, he is, and forever he will be.

Twenty-First Century Marys

There is no question as to the value of women in the Kingdom of God. Women were vital members of Jesus' ministry in the New Testament. They were among his most loyal followers. Women continue to be essential to the plan of God. The enemy has made it a priority to destroy us since the fall. "I will put enmity between you and the woman, and between your offspring and her offspring" (Genesis 3:15). "Satan hates women and has tried for centuries to destroy womanhood" (Piper and Grudem 2006, 390). Women are exploited, used, and abused, problems that continue to plague society.

Quite a few women in the Old Testament were described as beautiful in face and form. In their memoirs, none were described as having lives of ease and success. They had appearances other women envied, yet they were not content. Some wanted what they did not have. Others used their beauty for personal gain. Some of these women of beauty found themselves in compromising positions through no fault of their own. These women's lives included disobedience and sin. Here today, these beautiful women would no doubt be top models earning millions of dollars.

In contrast, women in the New Testament were rarely described as beautiful in face and form. Beauty was found in godly character and lives devoted to serving Christ and his church. Those extraordinary women of God who were included in the pages of the New Testament were motivated by love for Christ and a determination to serve and honor him with their lives. They supported Christ's ministry and helped to build and sustain the early church. Christ acknowledged and valued them as his faithful followers.

Women are continually in the spotlight. Beauty of face and form earn women fame and fortune. They not only allow it, but join with the world in exploiting themselves for personal and financial gain. Bare bodies and inappropriate clothing acquire unwanted attention. Yet that is not a deterrent to women who buy into the worldview. Fame and fortune are sought at the cost of devaluing femininity. We live in a culture that insists women are less valuable than men. Women are used and abused daily, degrading us even further. Girls from a very young age are bombarded by the world view. In spite of it, God is raising up godly women to reflect his character to the world around us. Beautiful women are used to convince us that our worth is found in appearance. We are continually bombarded by the worldview that the right education, career, money, clothing, shoes, and accessories will bring success and esteem. The truth is neither worth, success, nor is contentment found in outward sources, circumstances, millions of dollars on fashion and beauty products, or material things. Our worth, success, and contentment can only be found in Christ.

Mary of Bethany was an extraordinary woman who learned at an early age that Christ was her sole source of hope. Her faith and loyalty were evidenced in her behavior toward him. Some of her friends, relatives and neighbors hated Christ. She never wavered in her loyalty to him. She never gave into societal pressures. She is a great example for those of us who seek to honor Christ with our lives in a world that hates the things of God and everything and everyone who stands for him. Genuine success is measured in a continuing, growing relationship with Christ, persevering in faith and in service to him.

"Never be lacking in zeal, but keep your spiritual fervor, serving the Lord."
(Romans 12:11)

Chapter 9

A Servant's Heart

"Now as they went on their way, Jesus entered a village. And a woman named Martha welcomed him into her house" (Luke 10:38). Luke speaks of the house as Martha's house. Her name was usually listed first when she was named with her siblings. These two things together suggest she was the older sister. "Some believe Martha's position as owner of the house and dominate one in the household indicates she must have been a widow" (MacArthur, 2005, 157). While that is a possibility, there is no indication that she was married. All we know from Scripture is that the three siblings, Martha, Lazarus, and Mary lived together. There is no mention of any of them having been married, nor is there any definitive information about their ages. Based on significant assumptions, Martha appears to be the oldest of the three siblings. She appears practical, very hard working, and a very capable hostess. Martha may have bordered on perfectionism. However, the more probable reason for her activity was to give her best to her guest of honor. Regardless of her reason, the more important issue was overlooked. "And she had a sister called Mary, who sat at the Lord's feet and listened to his teaching. But Martha was distracted with much serving" (Luke 10:39-40a). Martha's priority was service. She no doubt loved Jesus and wanted to prepare and serve the best meal possible for her honored guest. Martha's behavior appeared to be that of a true servant. "And she went up to him and said, 'Lord, do you not care that my sister has left me to serve alone?' 'Tell her then to help me'" (Luke 10:40b). What Martha was doing was not a bad thing. She was serving Christ and her other guests. She began with the best motives and intentions. "But the Lord answered her, 'Martha, Martha, you are anxious and troubled about many things, but one thing is necessary. Mary has chosen the good portion, which will not be taken from her'" (Luke 10:41). Martha was so focused on service that she stopped listening to Christ and her perspective became self-centered and prideful. Her self-centered pride led her directly into sin. The result was anger, resentment, a critical spirit, jealousy, unkindness, and a judgmental spirit. Jesus' rebuke was kind and gentle. "Jesus did not condemn Martha's work, but her excessive attention to material provision, which disturbed her peace of mind and robbed her of the benefit of receiving the Lord's instruction" (Tenney 1976 [1975], 103). Good deeds, human charity, and acts of kindness are expressions of real faith, but they must flow from an authentic reliance on God's redemption and righteousness. Our good works can never be a means of earning God's favor. The focus of our faith is not what we do for God, but what he has done for us.

"At a second event, Martha's brother, Lazarus had been dead for four days. Martha met Jesus in the road where they had a discussion about death and resurrection and Jesus' identity" (Alexander 2009, 608). "So when Martha heard that Jesus was coming, she went and met him…Martha said to Jesus, 'Lord, if you had been here, my brother would not have died. But now I know that whatever you ask from God, God will give you'" (John 11:21-22). Martha went from a distracted servant to a believer. Christ's earlier rebuke of Martha did not alter her love and devotion for him. In fact, Christ's loving and merciful rebuke obviously got her attention. "Jesus said to her, 'Your brother will rise again.' Martha said to him, 'I know that he will rise again in the resurrection on the last day'" (John 11:23-24). Martha was versed in Scripture. She knew about the resurrection on the last day. Martha understood to a point. "Martha followed traditional patterns, worked hard and took her theology lesson at the moment it became relevant, while standing in the road. And the Holy Spirit revealed to her the profoundest truth" (Alexander 2009, 609). "Jesus said to her, 'I am the resurrection and the life. Whoever believes in me, though he die, yet shall he live, and everyone who lives and believes in me, shall never die. Do you believe this'" (John 11:25-26)? Martha was at a critical point. Martha loved Jesus. Her heart was broken with grief, and she sought hope and comfort in Christ. "She said to him, 'Yes, Lord; I believe that you are the Christ, the Son of God, who is coming into the world'" (John 11:27). Martha made a profession of faith. She had discovered the one thing needful: true worship and devotion of the heart and full attention to Christ.

"Six days before the Passover, Jesus therefore came to Bethany, where Lazarus was, whom Jesus had raised from the dead. So they gave a dinner for him there. Martha served" (John 12:1-2a). The passages in Luke 10:40

and John 12:2a both use the word serve in describing Martha's activity. The word serve in the Greek language, diakôneō, means to be an attendant, i.e. wait upon (menially of as a host, friend or teacher); as a deacon; minister (unto), serve, use the office of a deacon (NASB 1977 [1960], 22). Considering Martha's spiritual growth from the events describing the supper at Martha's house and in the book of John, the supper six days before the Passover, the application of the action of service would certainly have been different. In the first event where Martha was serving, she became indignant that her sister, Mary was not helping her. In the second event, Martha was preparing and serving in the same manner. Yet this time, there is no mention of her having a negative demeanor. She had previously acknowledged Jesus as the Christ, the Son of God. She witnessed Christ raise her brother, Lazarus from the dead. Martha was not the same woman. Serving Christ became an act of worship, done in love and adoration for the One in whom she believed to be her Savior.

Twenty-First Century Servants

Jesus said, "For it is written, 'You shall worship the Lord your God and him only shall you serve'" (Matthew 4:10). Serve in the Greek language here is latrĕuō, meaning render religious homage, serve, do the service, worship (NASB 1977 [1960], 44). Shall is an active future tense imperatival verb, meaning an active command in future time, a continual action. Christ describes service as an act of worship in an attitude of honor, respect, and reverence for God. Only is an adjective meaning alone, solitary. We are commanded to continually serve God and only God with honor and reverence in a constant sacrificial act of worship.

The view of service can be distorted. Service over relationship with God is not an act of worship and is counterproductive. It is not God honoring and hinders personal spiritual growth. Service can be used as a means of self-promotion, done in pride. Jesus said, "For I tell you, unless your righteousness exceeds that of the scribes and Pharisees, you will never enter the kingdom of heaven" (Matthew 5:20). "Pharisees were a legal party among the Jews who in their zeal for the Law they almost defiled it and their attitude became merely external, formal and mechanical" (Vine 1996 [1984], 470). Self-serving service is sinful. Service in an effort to earn God's favor is impossible. Salvation cannot be earned. "But if it is by grace, it is no longer on the basis of works; otherwise grace would no longer be grace" (Romans 11:6).

Service through Sanctification

"What good is it my brothers, if someone says he has faith but does not have works? Can faith save him" (James 2:14)? Yes! Faith in Jesus Christ, accepting him as Savior and Lord of our lives is sure and certain salvation. Salvation cannot be lost. Once saved, always saved. We are not saved by works. Works is an outpouring of faith. "Show me your faith apart from your works and I will show you my faith by my works…You see that faith was active along with works, and faith was completed by his works" (James 2:18b, 22). Works should be evidence of faith. We serve because we love the Lord, and from sincere gratitude for what he has done for us in saving us from our sin. Service in the Lord's name is giving of time, talents, gifts, and resources to him for the benefit of the Kingdom.

"Therefore, do not throw away your confidence, which has great reward. For you have need of endurance, so that when you have done the will of God, you may receive what is promised" (Hebrews 10:35-36). Christians have the assurance of heaven. Confidence in Christ and perseverance in faith carries present rewards in peace and joy. Perseverance also carries future rewards, for there will be rewards in heaven. "I the Lord search the heart and test the mind, to give every man according to the fruit of his deeds" (Jeremiah 17:10). "Whatever you do, work heartily as for the Lord and not for men, knowing that from the Lord you will receive the inheritance as your reward. You are serving the Lord Christ" (Colossians 3:23-24). How dreadful it would be to arrive at the judgment seat of Christ to receive awards for our service to him and have little to lie at his feet. Sanctification is a lifelong process of growing in Christ and being made in his image. It is not about the beginning, but the end. The ultimate goal is to end well. Our hope, our desire is to hear the Master say, "Well done, good and faithful servant" (Matthew 25:21). Like so many who have gone before us, may we end well.

"Therefore, go and make disciples of all nations, baptizing them in the name of the Father and of the Son and of the Holy Spirit, and teaching them to obey everything I have commanded you."
(Matthew 28:19-20)

Chapter 10

The First Evangelist

"Soon afterward he went on through the cities and villages, proclaiming and bringing the good news of the kingdom of God. And the twelve were with him, and also some women who had been healed of evil spirits and infirmities: Mary called Magdalene, from whom seven demons who had gone out, and Joanna the wife of Chuza, Herod's household manager, and Susanna, and many others who provided for them out of their means" (Luke 8:1-3). The most prominent of the women who accompanied Jesus from Galilee to Jerusalem, Mary Magdalene, is named in all four Gospels as a witness to his crucifixion, burial, and resurrection. "She came from Magdala, a tiny fishing village located on the northwest shore of the Sea of Galilee, some two or three miles north of the Roman city of Tiberius, and about five and a half miles south and west from Capernaum" (MacArthur 2005, 173). She was called Mary Magdalene to differentiate her from the other Mary's in the Bible.

Mary Magdalene's biography begins as a woman possessed by seven demons. "Demon possession involves bondage to an evil spirit-a real, personal, fallen spirit creature- that indwells the afflicted individual" (MacArthur 2005, 174). People who were demon-possessed were tormented and suffered greatly at the hands of these evil spirits. Mary Magdalene was tortured by seven demons. She was a prisoner of demonic afflictions. She was in perpetual agony. There is no information on how she became demon possessed, how long she lived that way, or how she met Jesus. There is no incidence recorded of any demon possessed individual having sought out Jesus for healing as did those with diseases and infirmities. The demon possessed lived as outcasts, forgotten by family and friends. Those possessed by demons were avoided. They were insolent and resistant toward Jesus. They never sought him out for help. It is significant that Jesus sought them out and healed them. Scripture doesn't give details concerning Mary Magdalene's demonic possession. However, her condition was extreme and probably one deemed completely beyond hope. Scripture does not reveal how or when she was delivered. "Jesus brought an abrupt end to her savage bondage, restored her to her right mind, and freed her to follow him" (Custis James 2005, 187). After Jesus delivered her, instead of sending her on her way, he brought her into his fellowship of followers. "She became part of a privileged group of women from Galilee who, along with the twelve disciples, accompanied Jesus as he traveled and ministered from town to town. Mary had a front row seat for Jesus' ministry and teaching" (Custis James 2005, 188).

Mary Magdalene is one of the most significant women in the New Testament. In all four of the Gospels, she is identified as one of Jesus' most devoted followers. If anyone doubts the significance of women in the Kingdom of God, Mary Magdalene's life is definitive proof to the contrary. Of the women who knew Jesus, only Mary of Nazareth is mentioned more times than Mary Magdalene.

She had a face to face relationship with Jesus and became a key contributor to the advancement of the kingdom. That she traveled with Jesus indicates that she was not married and had no familial responsibilities. She had some material resources and used them for Jesus because the group of women who traveled with Jesus not only cared for him and his disciples in practical ways, but also financed their travels.

Mary Magdalene remained a faithful disciple when others forsook him. She followed him all the way from Galilee to Jerusalem all the way to the cross and beyond. "But standing by the cross of Jesus were his mother and his mother's sister, Mary the wife of Clopas, and Mary Magdalene" (John 19:25). John was the only one of the eleven disciples remaining at the cross with the women. When John, the beloved disciple took Mary, the mother of Jesus away from the crucifixion sight, Mary Magdalene remained. This wasn't a safe place to be. Yet she remained faithful to the end. Joseph of Arimathea asked Pilate for the lifeless body of Jesus. Jesus' body was given to Joseph, and he laid it in a tomb, which was closed by rolling a great stone to cover the entrance of the tomb. Jesus' body was quickly anointed with spices and bound with linen cloths in preparation for burial before the Sabbath began. "Mary Magdalene and the other Mary were there, sitting opposite the tomb" (Matthew 27:61). It would have been these women who gave the disciples the description of how and where Jesus was buried. Mary Magdalene determined to return to the tomb the next morning to properly prepare the body of Christ with spices and ointments. Mary Magdalene, like the other disciples, had no thought of a resurrection. She had seen up close and personal the brutality of Jesus' death. She had seen his lifeless body buried in a tomb.

"Now on the first day of the week Mary Magdalene came to the tomb early, while it was still dark, and saw that the stone had been taken away from the tomb" (John 20:1). She ran to Peter and John, who ran back to the empty tomb. They saw the cloths lying there. Determining that the body had been stolen, they returned to their homes. But Mary Magdalene remained at the tomb and became the first person to witness the resurrected Christ. The first person Jesus appeared to and spoke to was a woman! After Jesus appeared to her, he sent her to proclaim the news that she had seen the risen Lord. Mary Magdalene became the first evangelist. "As the first person to meet the risen Jesus, and the first to be sent to tell others, Mary Magdalene is the 'apostle to the apostles' and so a critically important figure in early Christianity" (Alexander 2009, 640).

Jesus' resurrection is the central event of Christianity. Everything we believe hinges on this event. "One of the first matters of business when Jesus appeared to his male disciples was to establish the testimony of the women" (Cutis James 2005, 199). He had already elevated women by including them as his disciples, now he affirmed their ministries as his messengers.

Twenty-First Century Disciples

Women were not only support staff, they were crucial to Jesus' ministry. They did not have insignificant, obscure jobs or busy work. Mary Magdalene was given two of the most significant endorsements in Christ's ministry as the first witness to his resurrection and in having been sent to tell his disciples the good news of his resurrection from death. Women were there and were eye witnesses to the Christ, and his Great Commission is not gender specific. God allows us to be involved in his work to evangelize the world. Men and women are called to join together in service to Christ.

It is imperative that we understand salvation. Salvation is freely offered to all but it is dependent upon repentance of sin and faith in Christ. Salvation is the beginning of a relationship with Christ, a journey of sanctification, becoming one with Christ and in his likeness. "The Spirit himself bears witness with our spirit that we are children of God, and if children, then heirs-heirs of God and fellow heirs with Christ, provided we suffer with him in order that we may be glorified with him" (Romans 8:16-17). "The heirs of God presents a vivid view of the intimate and eternal union between the believer and God, and of the faithful soul's possession in present reality, and not merely in anticipation of the Kingdom of God on earth and in heaven" (Unger 1985 [1957], 619). As believers and followers of Christ, it is not about what we have done - the past is the past. The mistakes, the sin, the guilt is past. It is about what we are doing now and what we will do in the future for the Lord. "For God is not unjust so as to overlook your work and the love you have shown for his name in serving the saints, as you still do" (Hebrews 6:10). God sees all. Nothing escapes God's sight. Salvation guarantees heaven. Believers will face the judgment seat where we will be rewarded according to our works for Christ. "Rewards are offered by God to a believer on the basis of faithful service rendered after salvation" (Unger 1985 [1957], 1080). "Therefore do not throw away your confidence, which has a great reward. For you have need of endurance, so that when you have done the will of God, you may receive what is promised" (Hebrews 10:35-36). Does it really matter in the scheme of things that women and men have different roles in ministry? All service matters and God keeps an accounting of our faithfulness. It is not about what we as women cannot do. It is about what we can do. Our business is to be about God's business, serving, enduring, and persevering faithfully to the end. When we face Jesus and offer our rewards to him, when he extends his nail scarred hand to receive them, will we be ashamed of our gifts? While there is still time, let us work while there is yet work to be done.

***"Serve wholeheartedly, as if you were serving the Lord, not men,
because you know that the Lord will reward everyone whatever good he does."
(Ephesians 6:7-8)***

Chapter Eleven

A First-Century Business Woman

"Paul's second missionary journey led his group to Philippi, which was a leading city of the district of Macedonia and a Roman colony" (Acts 16:12a). "On the Sabbath Paul and his group went outside the gate to the riverside, where they supposed there was a place of prayer, and they sat down and spoke to the women who had come together" (Acts 16:13). "One who heard us was Lydia, from the city of Thyatira, a seller of purple goods, who was a worshipper of God. The Lord opened her heart to pay attention to what was said by Paul. And after she was baptized, and her household as well, she urged us, saying,

'If you have judged me to be faithful to the Lord, come to my house and stay'" (Acts 16:14-15).

Our lives are not random journeys that develop as we progress, depending upon our circumstances. Each of us is on the path God has planned for us. Our paths are not determined by ourselves or others, and our lives do not progress as we choose. God planned our journey and he is carrying out his plan for our lives – a life that will result in our good and his glory. Nothing, nor anyone, the enemy nor we can prevent God from accomplishing his plan for our lives. The purpose of our lives is far greater than our personal fulfillment, our peace of mind, or even our happiness. It is far greater than our family, career, or our wildest dreams and ambitions. "If we want to know why we were placed on this earth, we must begin with God. We were born by his purpose and for his purpose" (Warren 2002, 17).

Lydia, although not European, is remembered as the first person on record ever to respond to the message of the gospel during the Apostle Paul's first missionary journey to Europe. "Because her home was Thyatira, located on the confines of Lydia and Mysia in Asia Minor, her name probably was common in that general area. Thyatira was a city of dye-makers, especially famous for purple from the shellfish Purpura Murex. Lydia could have been in Philippi temporarily selling her wares from her home town" (Couch 1999, 331). Thyatira had been famous for centuries for its dyeing industry and production of purple dyed garments that were highly prized and costly. "Lydia, herself, specialized in cloth treated with an expensive purple dye and was presumably the Macedonian agent of a Thyatiran manufacturer" (Stott 1990, 263). Lydia was a business woman, not Jewish, and not European. Apparently Lydia was a widow. Her household is mentioned, but there is no mention of her husband. She may have carried on the business for her deceased husband. Her household could have been comprised of children, slaves, or servants. "The Gentile proselyte Lydia was a worshipper of God in the Old Testament sense" (Couch 1999, 331).

The men having gone outside the gate to the riverside to pray suggest there was no synagogue in the city. "The lack of a synagogue meant there were very few Jews, for it took only ten Jewish men to constitute a synagogue. No number of women could compensate for the absence of even one man necessary to complete the quorum of ten" (Couch 1999, 330). "According to Jewish tradition, in communities without synagogues, Jewish women could pray together in groups if they wished. They could not participate in any type of formal, public or communal worship – including prayer, reading the Torah, or the giving of public blessings" (MacArthur 2005, 190).

A group of women had gone outside the city, to the riverside to pray. Because there was no synagogue, Paul and his companions went outside the city to the riverside where prayer was customarily made. They sat down and spoke to the women who met there. There they met Lydia. Lydia had a divine appointment with God. A woman's highest calling and deepest need is to know God. Lydia was a seeker of God. "Seeking God and trusting Christ is not merely a decision that lies within the power of our own will to choose, nor are we sovereign over our own heart and affections. When we see a soul like Lydia's truly seeking God, we can be certain God is calling her" (MacArthur 2005, 1992). The Bible tells us that as Lydia listened, the Lord opened her heart. Lydia listened intently. Her attention was honed in as Paul explained the gospel message. The Lord opened her heart to understand and accept the message of Christ. It was God who gave her the ears to hear. It was God who gave her the eyes to see Jesus. It was God who opened her heart to accept God's gift of faith in Christ. God clearly orchestrated the circumstances that brought Paul to Macedonia. In his sovereignty, God placed Lydia there, drew her to the riverside to pray and gave her a seeking, hungry heart. She instantly responded to the message of Christ, became a believer, and was baptized then and there. Lydia's entire household came to faith and were baptized that same morning.

Lydia's conversion is evidenced in her hospitality to the missionaries as she invited the entire entourage to stay in her home. She offered to house them indefinitely. This would have been a daunting task as we know the group included Paul, Timothy, Silas, Luke, and possibly others. Lydia's home became the base for the missionary team. "Lydia's hospitality opened the way for the church to penetrate Europe" (MacArthur 2005, 196). As a result, a number of people responded to the gospel and their first meeting place was Lydia's home. This became the first church ever established in Europe.

The Twenty-First Century Response

"Draw near to God and he will draw near to you" (James 4:8). We are as close to God as we want to be. Like anything else, we get out of it what we put into it. It takes discipline, obedience, desire, time, and energy. God desires our all. "And you shall love the Lord your God with all your heart and with all your soul, with all your mind and with all your strength" (Mark 12:30). He wants all of us – our hearts, our souls, our minds and our strength. The ultimate goal of all of creation is to reveal the glory of God. It is the reason for everything in existence. Our first responsibility is to worship God and in our worship and honor, we bring glory to him.

If you want to know a person's priorities, look at their checkbooks. The most valued and important things in our lives are evidenced by the time, energy and resources we put into them. "When we give someone our time, we are giving a portion of our lives that we will never get back.

Our time is our lives and the greatest gift we can give" (Warren 2002, 127).

We were created to serve God. Everything that happens to us has spiritual significance – the good, the bad and the indifferent things. We were put here to make a difference, to make a contribution. Nothing that happens to us is insignificant. God uses all things to prepare us for eternity. He never wastes anything. It is all to be used for his benefit and glory. "Serve wholeheartedly, as if you were serving the Lord, not men, because you know that the Lord will reward everyone whatever good he does" (Ephesians 6:7-8). We are addicted to doing. We have become humans doing rather than humans being. We are so busy doing that we have little time for God. Our relationship with him suffers as a result. Our service to him becomes nonexistent. We do well just to attend church, and that may be sporadic. There is a significant difference between church goers and church members, and that is commitment. Church goers refuse to get involved. They have no motivation or desire to serve. Members, as a rule, get involved in the ministries of the church and serve even when it is not particularly enjoyable. Church goers are takers. Members are contributors in every sense of the word. Church goers want the benefits without the responsibility. Members gladly accept service as a responsibility. Service involves loving God and loving people. "You shall love your neighbor as yourself" (Matthew 19:19b). Jesus gave us a direct command. If we truly love God with all our hearts, souls, minds and strength, we will have no problem loving our neighbors. This means loving the unlovable. It means loving when we do not feel like it. It includes loving when we are not loved in return. It includes loving without expectation. Our treatment of others is an indicator of our genuine love for Christ. Our love for neighbor and Christ propels us to service to both. If everyone served, what a difference it would make in the church and in the kingdom of God. Service plugs us into the heartbeat of the church and we become an active part of God's plan for his church. Getting in on where God is working generates life changing benefits. We need to see ministry as an opportunity, rather than an obligation. It is in ministry that we find genuine significance and meaning. In putting others above ourselves responses and reactions to obstacles, trials and tribulations become less consuming. When our focus is outward rather than inward, our view of life is less intimidating. When our focus is on Christ, when our minds are positioned on living for him, everything else becomes less important. It's when trials of life take precedence that we sink in despair. When Christ is not our focus, we are more likely to make poor choices that affect not only ourselves but others.

Are we seekers of God? Are we living out our salvation? "Therefore, my dear friends, as you have always obeyed – not only in my presence, but now much more in my absence – continue to work our your salvation with fear and trembling, for it is God who works in you to will and to act according to his purpose" (Philippians 2:12-13). The key to living the Christian life is obedience. We must be vigilant concerning what we believe and in how we live. Our attention must be focused on Christ so we do not get distracted. We have one shot at life. At the end of yours, will you have made a difference?

"Therefore, I urge you, brothers, in view of God's mercy to offer your bodies as living sacrifices, holy and pleasing to God – this is your spiritual act of worship." (Romans 12:1)

Chapter Twelve

Givers and Takers

"Jesus looked up and saw the rich putting their gifts into the offering box, and he saw a poor widow put in two small copper coins." (Luke 21:1-2).

In the ancient Old Testament culture, a woman who survived her husband faced an uncertain future. If she had children, she could not inherit from her husband. Land passed from father to sons, the eldest son receiving twice as much as each of his brothers. If there were no sons, inheritance could pass to daughters. A widow could remain in the husband's family if the next of kin took her in marriage. "The Law of Levirate marriage (Deuteronomy 25:5-10) provided for widows in that if brothers (on the father's side) lived together, that is, in the same place, and one of them died childless, the wife was not to go outside the family to marry a stranger; but the surviving brother (kinsman redeemer) was to take her as his wife" (Unger 1985 [1957], 821). Often widows found themselves without financial support. Old Testament laws were established to protect widows, the fatherless, and the aliens (Deuteronomy 24:17-21). The fact that laws were made to protect widows from cruel treatment validates that such acts were common. "In the early church, money was set aside to care for widows (Acts 6:1), because in the society of the day, prostitution was about the only way for women to obtain money to live" (Gower 2005, 70). The scribes took advantage of this vulnerable group of women by taking advantage of them for selfish gain. "By the time the pastoral epistles were written, the Christian community had not changed its basic attitude toward widows, but experience was forcing some considerations" (Tenney 1976 [1975], 928). Qualifications were determined for widow's eligibility to receive distributions of charity. Life was especially difficult for widows. In this context, we can better grasp the significance of the contribution by the widow in the temple.

In the court of women, east of Herod's temple there were thirteen boxes for contributions brought by worshippers. Men and women were allowed in this court. Jesus was at the temple watching the rich putting their gifts in the treasury when he noticed a poor widow making a donation. She gave two very small copper coins. "These were thin, small, light copper coins, the smallest of Jewish coins. "And Jesus said, 'Truly I tell you, this poor widow has put in more than all of them. For they all contributed out of their abundance, but she out of her poverty put in all she had to live on'" (Luke 21:3-4). This poor widow gave everything she had placing complete dependence upon God for her provision. Of all those who gave, this poor widow was recognized by Jesus and became an example of a true sacrificial giver. Her act of faith evidences her belief and trust in the one true God.

Dorcas

"Now there was in Joppa a disciple named Tabitha, which translated, means Dorcas. She was full of good works and acts of charity. In those days she became ill and died, and when they had washed her, they laid her in an upper room" (Acts 9:36-37). Peter was in the vicinity, and two men were sent to urge him to return to Joppa with them. The disciples at Joppa had knowledge of the disciple's ministries and works and believed that Peter could raise their friend from the dead. Upon his arrival, Peter found that Dorcas was mourned by many. "And when he arrived, they took him to the upper room. All the widows stood beside him weeping and showing tunics and other garments that Dorcas made while she was with them" (Acts 9:39).

"Joppa was an important Christian center during the years when the new faith was spreading from Jerusalem across the Mediterranean" (Deen 1983, 218). Her acts of charity indicate that Dorcas was a woman of means. However, her charity did not include only purchasing fabric for making tunics and garments for those in need; she gave her time and energy in creating the clothing. Dorcas was a true servant who loved God and loved people. Peter recognized her selfless contribution to the cause of Christ. "Peter put them all outside, and knelt down and prayed, and turning to the body said, 'Tabitha, arise.' And when she opened her eyes, and when she saw Peter, she sat up. And he gave her his hand and raised her up" (Acts 9:40-41). Peter used the Aramaic form of Dorcas' name. There is no indication why Peter used her Aramaic name. It is not of significance in this study other than for clarification purposes. This miracle was the first of its kind performed by an apostle. The news of Dorcas spread all over Joppa, and many believed as a result. There is little doubt that the witness and ministry of Dorcas that followed drew many more to faith in Christ.

Phoebe

"I commend to you sister Phoebe, a servant of the church at Cenchreae, that you may welcome her in the Lord in a way worthy of the saints, and help her in whatever she may need from you, for she has been a patron of many and of myself as well" (Romans 16:1-2). Phoebe's name appears once in the New Testament, but that does not diminish the role she played in the early church. Her contributions give further evidence to the value of women in the early Christian church. "Phoebe may have been the one entrusted with the mission of delivering Paul's letter, written at Corinth, a city near Cenchreae, to Rome. In referring to her as a deaconess and helper, Paul used terms that may have indicated offices or ministries by which Phoebe served the larger church" (Gardner 1994, 358).

"The word servant comes from the Greek word diakŏnŏs, from which the word deacon is derived. Translated in the Greek language, this word means attendant, waiter, servant, minister, teacher and pastor" (NASB 1977 [1960], 22). Many commentators have surmised that Phoebe was a deaconess. From a Biblical point of view, we know that women were not deacons or pastors in the early church. The Doctrine of Headship prohibits women from holding the office of pastor, elder, or deacon. This is not to minimize the fundamental ministry of women and their key contributions to the early church in acts of ministry, charity, and hospitality. In Paul's usage, servant likely implies that, as his patroness, Phoebe assisted him physically and financially. "Phoebe probably had some wealth and position, or she could not have traveled about as she did" (Deen 1955, 231). "When Paul asked the Romans to 'help her in whatever she may need from you,' she may have been raising financial support for Paul, perhaps for the long-planned mission of which the apostle had written just before introducing Phoebe: 'I will leave for Spain by way of you'" (Gardner 1994, 358). Paul's introduction of Phoebe as a saint evidences his distinctive relationship with her. His declaration that Phoebe had been a patron of many as well as himself indicates that Phoebe's service was significant and extensive. We can conclude that the early church flourished because of the ministries, contributions, and services of women.

Sapphira

Sapphira and her husband Ananias were members of the early Christian church at Jerusalem. "And all who believed were together and had all things in common. And they were selling all their possessions and belongings and distributing the proceeds to all, as many as had need" (Acts 2:44-45). "There was not a needy person among them, for as many as were owners of lands or houses sold them and brought the proceeds of what was sold and laid it at the apostles' feet, and it was distributed to each as any had need" (Acts 4:34-35). Sapphira and Ananias agreed with others to share all that they had with one another and to contribute to a common fund that was divided by the apostles among the poor. Ananias and Sapphira possessed land and sold it for the purpose of contributing to the cause. They were not forced to sell their possessions nor were they required to give up all their property. After they sold the property, they were not required to give up all the proceeds. The proceeds were given strictly on a voluntary basis. "But a man named Ananias, with his wife Sapphira, sold a piece of property, and with his wife's knowledge he kept back for himself some of the proceeds and brought only a part of it and laid it at the apostle's feet" (Acts 5:1-2). The issue here is not that Ananias and Sapphira only gave a portion of the proceeds from the sale of their land. The problem is why they withheld it. "As members of the Christian community, they voluntarily made an agreement, and this agreement became a sacred pledge for the faithful" (Deen 1983, 213). But amid all the noble ideas Sapphira and her husband had, they become more interested in what they had than in what they were. Sapphira and her husband held back part of the proceeds from the sale of the land and brought the pretended price to the apostle Peter. There is no record of Sapphira having tried to dissuade her husband in this lie. To the contrary, Scripture is clear that Sapphira was entirely complicit in the act, making her equally guilty. The guilt lay in their greediness, their lack of integrity and their having postulated themselves among the selfless who had given what they had vowed to give. "Peter said to Ananias, 'Why is it that you have contrived this deed in your heart? You have not lied to men, but to God'" (Acts 5:4b). The church now numbered about five thousand. "The ushering in of a new era of Pentecost necessitated that offenders against divine dealings in grace might be made a public example" (Unger 1985 [1957], 57). When Ananias had no answer, he fell dead at Peter's feet, and was taken out and buried. Three hours later, Sapphira appeared before Peter and he inquired of her as to the amount of the sale of their property. Scripture reveals she had no prior knowledge of the fate of her husband. Her answer to Peter's question reveals her complicity in her and her husband's cover-up. Her lie resulted in immediate death and she was taken out and buried beside her husband. While this seems rather harsh, the sudden death of Sapphira and Ananias made others in the church aware that God does not tolerate sin. "No one can serve two masters, for either he will hate the one and love the other, or he will be devoted to one and despise the other. You cannot serve God and money" (Matthew 6:24). Word of the incident spread and people from the cities around Jerusalem came and were healed of sickness and unclean spirits. Fear fell upon the people and believers came forward in multitudes. Sapphira and her husband are examples of sin, its selfish desires, and its consequences. "Do not lay up for yourselves treasures on earth, where moth and rust destroy and where thieves break in and steal, but lay up for yourselves treasures in heaven, where neither moth nor rust destroys and where thieves do not break in and steal. For where your treasure is, there your heart is also" (Matthew 6:19-21).

Twenty-First Century Givers and Takers

"Judge not, and you will not be judged, condemn not and you will not be condemned; forgive and you will be forgiven; give and it will be given to you. Good measure, pressed down, shaken together, running over, will be put into your lap. For the measure you use it will be measured back to you" (Luke 6:37-38). God requires our service, our giving of financial resources, and our spiritual growth. Out of spiritual growth emerges a hunger for Christ, a desire to serve and a spirit of generosity to give back to God a portion of the financial resources he has granted us. God promises compounded returns for our obedience to him.

Failure to do so will result in attitudes that render us useless for the kingdom of God. Judgmental, unforgiving, selfish attitudes stifle spiritual growth and encourage discontent, financial insecurity, condemnation, insecurity, and failure. "A woman's theology, regardless of what shape it is in, affects others" (Custis James 2001, 169). What we believe about God impacts others either positively or negatively. Our attitudes and actions are to reflect the heart and mind of Christ. We please God by what we believe as well as what we do. Our obedience is evidence of our love for Christ. Service and stewardship go hand in hand. "Servant in Greek language, "doulos" (δοῦλος) used as a noun, is the most common and general word for "servant" frequently indicating subjection without the idea of bondage" (Vine, 1996 [1984], 562). "Servant in Greek language, "douloō" (δουλόω) used as a verb means to enslave, to bring into bondage" (Vine 1996 [1984], 563). In this context, service means being willingly brought into bondage to become a slave or servant of Christ. "Stewardship in Greek language, "oikonomos" (οἰκονόμος) used as a noun means primarily the manager of a house or estate, such were usually slaves or freedmen" (Vine 1996 [1984], 599). "Steward in Greek language, "oikonomeō" (οἰκονόμέω) used as a verb means to be a manager or superintendent of another's household" (Unger 1988 [1957], 1221. In this context, steward means believers are to be managers or superintendents of God. God expects our obedience in both. How are we handling the resources God has given us? "As each has received a gift, use it to serve one another, as good stewards of God's varied grace" (1 Peter 4:10). Our mission is significant. God uses passion to further his kingdom. Are we passionate about the things of God? We are exactly where we want to be. Without motivation, we become stagnant. Stagnation yields us up to slothfulness. "For whatever overcomes a person, to that he is enslaved" (2 Peter 2:19b). God is a gentleman. He never forces himself on anyone. He grants us freedom to choose whom we will serve. "If anyone serves me, he must follow me; and where I am, there will my servant be also. If anyone serves me, the Father will honor him" (John 12:26). Heaven is in store for all believers. What we do on this side of eternity determines the rewards we will receive in glory. "So then each of us will give an account of himself to God" (Romans 14:12). When we fully comprehend that there is more to life than what we perceive in the present, we will begin to live in light of eternity.

"Now to him who is able to do far more abundantly than all we ask or think, according to the power at work within us, to him be glory in the church and in Christ Jesus throughout all generations, forever and ever."
(Ephesians 3:20-21)

Chapter Thirteen

Female Leadership in the Early Church

"Greet Priscilla and Aquila, my fellow workers in Christ Jesus. They risked their lives for me. Not only I but all the churches of the Gentiles are grateful to them" (Romans 16:3-16). Priscilla and Aquila were Jewish natives from Pontus. Pontus was a large district in northern Asia Minor where there were many Jewish residents. At times, those in Palestine seemed to have suffered much persecution by the governors. About the middle of his reign, all Jews who lived in Rome were driven out by Claudius Caesar's anti-Semitic decree. Aquila and Priscilla were among those who left Italy because of this edict of the emperor Claudius Caesar. They relocated to Corinth where they met Paul. "Since they, like Paul, were tent makers, the apostle lived and worked with them while he was in Corinth. They became part of his entourage and accompanied him when he left Corinth for Ephesus, where the church met in their house" (Gardner 1994, 46). They traveled with Paul to Ephesus where Paul left them. When Paul returned a year or so later, he found a well-established and organized church. Priscilla, together with her husband, played a very important role in the early Christian church. Their relationship with Paul was significant as suggested by his mention of them several times in his writings.

Priscilla was willing to make sacrifices in the spreading of the gospel at a time when Christians faced a great persecution. She worked as a tent maker, managed her home where the church met, and was obviously a thorough student of the gospel. She was a virtuous woman sharing with others the knowledge God had given her. An example of this is found in her encounter with Apollos. "Now a Jew named Apollos, a native of Alexandria, came to Ephesus. He was an eloquent man, competent in the Scriptures" (Acts18:24). Apollos spoke boldly and accurately concerning the things he knew about Jesus. However, Apollos had limited knowledge of the gospel. "He began to speak boldly in the synagogue, but when Priscilla and Aquila heard him, they took him and explained to him "the way of God more accurately'" (Acts 18:26). Priscilla was noted for her hospitality and she and Aquila possibly took Apollos into their home while they trained him. Because of their willingness and efforts in teaching and training him in the truth of the gospel, Apollos became an articulate and effective Christian teacher and missionary. "This is helpful evidence that informal discussion of Scripture by men and women together, in which both men and women play a significant role in helping one another understand Scripture, is approved by the New Testament. This example cautions us not to prohibit activities which are not prohibited in Scripture, yet it does not overturn the principle that the publically recognized governing and teaching role within a church is restricted to men" (Grudem 1994, 943). Priscilla was a theologian. "Theology is the study of God, divine things and religious truth" (Webster 2001, 814). As women, we are challenged to take responsibility for the personal studying of Scripture and how its truth applies to our lives. "Biblical theology is the study of the teaching of the individual authors and sections of the Bible and of the place of each teaching in the historical development of the Bible" (Grudem 1994, 1237). Priscilla had a career and managed her home. The church met and grew in her home. She, with Aquila taught and trained Apollos in the truth of God's word and sent him out into the world to spread the gospel. She used what she had for the glory of God, for his Church, and for his mission, without restriction and disobedience to her submission to headship. Amid persecution, she persevered, unwilling to waiver in her service.

Paul gives credence to several women in the 16th Chapter of Romans other than Phoebe and Priscilla. Mary is one of six in the New Testament. She is virtually unknown other than mention of her in verse six. Junias was imprisoned with Paul and considered outstanding by the apostles. Tryphena, Tryphosa, Persis, the mother of Rufus, Julia, and Nereus' sister were acknowledged in Paul's catalog of personal greetings as fellow workers for the Lord, personal friends of Paul and saints of the Lord. The very fact that these women are mentioned gives validity to their invaluable contribution to the early church.

Twenty-First Century Theologians

Nowhere are we told that women cannot be theologians. In fact, the Bible persuades women to become students of Scripture. The kingdom is in desperate need of women who are seekers of the truth and knowledgeable about Scripture. The kingdom is in desperate need of women of the Word who are willing to pour their lives into others to teach and train them the truth of Scripture. Self-help books and quick fixes have become the go to for answers and help in times of need. The Bible is the most accurate and complete instruction book on surviving and thriving in this world. So many times we miss the mark. We get it wrong because we do not give the time or make the effort to seek truth. Women have become disillusioned. Our roles in the church and where we fit in the kingdom have become confusing. In one respect, we women are taught we have limitations in ministry in the church. In the other respect, we are told women have no limitations in ministry in the church. We are bombarded with the worldview of equality and women's rights. We have bought into the idea that men are superior to women and we deserve equal treatment, equal pay, equal rights, and equal opportunities. We are looking for answers in all the wrong places. Jesus was continually challenged by the Pharisees and Sadducees as to his authority. "But Jesus answered them, 'You are wrong, because you know neither the Scriptures nor the power of God'" (Matthew 22:29). On so many occasions, we women are misled because we know neither the Scriptures nor the power of God. Theology has been a man's game, not because of any mandates, but because we have left that responsibility to them. Whether we acknowledge it or not, whether we are aware of it or not, we are theologians. Theology is the study of God. "Systematic theology is any study that answers the question, 'What does the whole Bible teach us today?' about any given topic'" (Grudem 1994, 1255). The accurate, persistent and thorough study of Scripture makes it possible for us to be obedient to Christ and to teach others the truth of the gospel and its benefits for individuals, the family of God and the world at large.

Theology is meant to be lived. What we believe, how we live reveals our understanding of God. Our theology either draws others to him or fails to initiate any interest in him. What we believe, how we live affects others. We must not be dependent on others as our sole inspiration and authority on Scripture. We do need theologically sound teaching from others, but also involvement and commitment in Christ's church, and taking responsibility for personal Bible study and prayer.

"Now to him who is able to do far more abundantly than all we ask or think, according to the power at work within us, to him be glory in the church and in Christ Jesus throughout all generations, forever and ever" (Ephesians 3:20-21). The power within us is the Spirit of God, the same Spirit of God who raised Jesus from the dead. This power enables us to become all we were created to be, without excuse, reason, or hindrance. The truth is we are here because God ordained it. The directions our lives have taken are not by happenstance. The direction our lives have taken is purposed. Life is not about what we deserve. Though we are undeserving, Christ came, suffered, died and rose again to give us a heavenly hope and future. Our service and ministry is not based on what we deserve, what we can get from it, or what we can or cannot do in ministry. It must be based on our great love, devotion and gratitude to Christ for all that he has done for us. Our roles as women are not based on equality or worth by the world's standards. Our roles, equality, and worth are based on and founded in Christ. Our ministry in the church is based on our love, devotion and commitment to Christ. Our responsibility is to know Christ, not know about him, but to know him and to have a developing relationship with him. Only in seeking God with our whole hearts can we truly know him. Only by becoming women of the Word can we have knowledge of him. Only by becoming women of prayer can we understand him and develop and maintain an intimate relationship with him. There is one hindrance to our successes and victories as women. That hindrance is a personal choice. What we do with Christ is no one else's responsibility. What we do with Christ is no one else's decision. What we fail to do with Christ is no one else's fault or excuse. The decision is ours alone. The results are ours alone.

The Bible is an all-inclusive instruction book for navigating through life on earth, preparing us for eternity along the journey. The Bible is God's love letter to us. Women are his special, unique, and amazing gift in his creation and purpose. His purpose for our lives is not some illusive, entangled puzzle in which we have the daunting task to determine where and how we fit into the kingdom plan. God's will for our lives is for us to know him, to have a relationship with him, to grow into the likeness of Christ as we journey through life in preparation for eternity. Any service and ministry we do for God is a blessed privilege and opportunity to honor him and give him glory. Women are ministers in every respect of the word. Any restrictions women have under the Doctrine of Headship are for our protection. Headship is by God's design and our responsibility to God is to live in obedience to that doctrine. Obedience to headship whether to father, husband, or church leadership affords women exhaustive opportunities to serve and to minister. "God has given much insight and wisdom to women as well as to men, and any church leaders who neglect to draw on the wisdom that women have are acting foolishly (Grudem 1994, 944). Together, men and women can change the world for the glory of God. In Christ alone we find complete confidence, contentment, satisfaction, love and worth. There is nothing greater, and no greater message to share with the world.

Conclusion

Where do we begin? Here and now is the birthplace of beginning. Consider for a moment where you are. Take inventory of your life. If you are like many women, your inventory is a listing of negatives that represent faults, regrets, failures, sorrows, lost hopes and dreams. For a moment, forget what was, what could have been, what happened, what did not happen, the regrets, the failures, the sorrows, the lost hopes and dreams. Although seemingly impossible, empty your minds of the ever spinning thoughts, responsibilities, and never ending to-do lists. The earth will not stop spinning on its axis if you let go and completely relax your mind, body and spirit for a moment.

How do we begin? On your inventory list, make note of where you would like to be in the here and now. Determine to set goals for yourself. Obtaining goals does not have to be improbable or impossible. However, achieving goals requires change. Change has taken on quite a negative and extensive inference. The daunting task of change is difficult and presents itself as insurmountable. Change takes place in the mind. It is an act of the will. Consider the possibilities change offers. Here is where we face that constant quandary of intense struggle - choice. Reconsider change. Change is nothing more than choice. We choose to allow change to control us or we choose to control our responses and reactions to change.

We all struggle with suffering and pain, illness, heartache, temptation, worry, anxiety, anger, forgiveness, lack, loneliness, depression, disappointment, regret, guilt and insecurities. No person, male or female, rich or poor, young or old, Chief Executive Officer or unemployed, educated or uneducated, privileged or underprivileged is immune. Life happens. We all react differently.

Victimized? We are victims only if we choose to be. We are held hostage by persons, things, or events simply because we give those persons, things or events the power to hold us hostage. We choose to give power to people, alcohol, drug, and sex addictions, sexual abuse, domestic abuse, and child abuse, poverty, stress, anxiety, depression, illness, forgiveness, anger, homosexuality- the list is endless. We can take the easy road to reason, excuse, and blame giving power to source and cause, avoiding taking personal responsibility or accountability.

When do we begin? There is no better time than now. Procrastination, laziness, and failure to follow through are bad habits to establish. It is easier to form a habit than break a habit. There is an adage that says it takes twenty-one days to form a habit and twenty-one days to break a habit. In reality, the length of time it takes to break a habit depends on the severity of the habit. Whatever the length of time required to break a habit, it is a small price to pay for freedom from bondage to those habits. Take the challenge to practice self-control. Tackle one habit at a time, one day at a time. Set reasonable goals for yourself. Take time to adjust and enjoy freedom and success before tackling another habit. Excess expectation sets us up for disappointment and failure.

To whom and what do we seek for help in the trials, temptations, and evils life continually hurls at us? Billions of dollars are spent on resources and treatments annually to help overcome habits and addictions, none of which guarantee success. The answer is simple. The answer requires no cost comparison shopping. The answer is not based on who we are, what we are, where we are, what we have done or have not done, our social status, or our health. Are you a smoker? Do you abuse alcohol, drugs, or people? Have you been accused or convicted of a crime? Perhaps you have been divorced - multiple times. Perhaps you struggle with infertility, or having had abortions. Perhaps your struggle is promiscuity or prostitution. Is your struggle food disorder related? Maybe your struggle is fear, anxiety, worry, anger, unforgiveness, hate, resentment, self-loathing, depression, or selfishness to name a few.

The answer is found in one source and it is free of charge to all people. The answer is tried, true and guaranteed. We desperately seek the answer in all the wrong places. The reality is that what we desperately need is the Bible, God's Holy Word. The reality is that who we desperately need is Jesus. Where and how do we find this Jesus? The Bible is God's instruction book for life. Find the map for hope below.

"For all have sinned and fall short of the glory of God" (Romans 3:23). We all have one commonality. We are sinners. All of us fall short of God's favor and there is absolutely nothing we can do in and of ourselves to change that.

"For the wages of sin is death" (Romans 6:23a). There is a penalty for sin. The penalty is death. Whether or not we believe it, death is not our final destination. Death precedes heaven or hell.

"But the free gift of God is eternal life in Jesus Christ our Lord" (Romans 6:23b). Jesus died to give us life. If you or I were the only one person in the world who was separated from God, Jesus would have died for that one person. In

Jesus, God offers the free gift of eternal life, the promise of heaven.

"But God shows his love for us in that while we were still sinners, Christ died for us" (Romans 5:8). The penalty for sin is death. Because of our sin and in spite of us, Christ chose to die for us. He chose to take the penalty for our sin upon himself.

"For everyone who calls on the name of the Lord will be saved" (Romans 10:13). Jesus accepts all of us, not based on who we are or what we have done. He accepts us on the basis of who he is and what he has done for us.

"Because if you confess with your mouth that Jesus is Lord and believe in your heart that God raised him from the dead, you will be saved" (Romans 10:9). Forgiveness cannot be earned. Salvation is a gift. Our responsibility in salvation is choosing to repent of our sin and believe in the One who came to save us.

"I appeal to you therefore, brothers, by the mercies of God, to present your bodies as a living sacrifice, holy and acceptable to God, which is your spiritual act of worship. Be not conformed to this world, but be transformed by the renewal of your mind, that by testing you may discern what is the will of God, what is good and acceptable and perfect" (Romans 12:1-2). Enough said.

We can find help for the trials, temptations and evils of life,

and encouragement for peace, joy and hope when faced

with uncertain days. The following chart is a useful guide:

Anger	Psalm 103:8. Proverbs 15:1, Ephesians 4:26, 4:31, Matthew 5:22
Backsliding	John 15:1-10, Hebrews 10:26-27, 35-38
Depression or illness	Psalm 23, 91, 34
Doubt	Matthew 17:20, John 20:25-28, James 1:6-8
Envy	James 3:14-16, Mark 7:20-22, 1 Cor. 13:4
Fear	Psalm 2:11, Proverbs 31:30, Isiah 41:10
Forgiveness, Forgiving	Luke 7:47-49, Matthew 6:14
Grace	Ephesians 2:5, 2 Timothy 1:8-9
Happiness	James 5:13, Psalm 32:1-2
Holiness	1 Peter 1:15-16,

	Romans 6:12-14
Humility	Colossians 3:12, 2:23
Judgmental	Luke 6:37-38, James 2:13
Kindness	Ephesians 4:32, 1 Thessalonians 5:15
Joy	Psalm 68:3, John 15:11, John 16:20, Gal. 5:22
Love	Matthew 22:37-39, 1 John 4:7-21,
Marriage	Ephesians 5:22-28, 33, Hebrews 13:4
Mercy	Micah 6:8, Luke 6:36, Titus 3:5
Money	Ecclesiastes 5:10, Matthew 6:24
Perseverance	Romans 5:3, James 1:3, 1:4
Pride	Proverbs 16:18, Galatians 6:1-6
Repentance	Isaiah 30:15, Acts 2:38,

	Revelation 3:19-20
Selfishness	Philippians 2:3-4, James 3:16
Suffering	Romans 5:3, Hebrews 2:10, 1 Peter 4:12
Temptation	Matthew 26:41, 1 Corinthians 10:13
The Tongue	Proverbs 21:23, James 1:26
Truth	John 14:6, John 16:13
Word of God	Proverbs 30:5-6, Revelation 22:18-19
Worldliness	1 John 2:15-17, Colossians 3:2, 23
Worry	Matthew 6:25-34, 1 Peter 5:7

Hope is found in Christ Jesus. In Christ, we find help, hope, courage, faith and strength to navigate through this journey we call life. "I pray that out of his glorious riches he may strengthen you with power through his Spirit in your inner being, so that Christ may dwell in your hearts through faith. And I pray that you, being rooted and established in love, may have power, together with all the saints, to grasp how wide and long and high and deep is the love of Christ, and to know this love that surpasses knowledge – that you may be filled to the measure of all the faithfulness of God. Now to him who is able to do immeasurably more than all we ask or imagine, according to his power that is at work in us, to him be glory in the church and in Christ Jesus throughout all generations, for ever and ever! Amen" (Ephesians 3:17b-21).

Reference List

Zodhiates, Spiros, Warren Baker, and Joel Kletzing, eds. 1977. *Hebrew-Greek Key Word Study Bible, New American Standard*. Tennessee: AMG Publishers. (Orig. pub. 1960).

MacArthur, John. 2005. *Twelve Extraordinary Women*. Tennessee: Thomas Nelson.

Clouse, Bonnidell and Robert G. Clouse, eds. 1989. *Women in Ministry*. Illinois: InterVarsity Press.

Custis James, Carolyn. 2005. *Lost Women if the Bible, The Women We Thought We Knew*. Michigan: Zondervan.

Geoffrey W. Bromiley, General Editor. 1986. *The International Standard Bible Encyclopedia*. Vol. 3. Michigan: William B. Eerdmans Publishing Co.

Henry, Matthew. 1984. *Commentary on the Whole Bible*. Vol. 2. New York: Fleming H. Revell Company.

LaSor, William Sanford, David Allan Hubbard, Frederic WM. Bush. 1987. *Old Testament Survey*. Michigan: William B. Eerdmans Publishing Company. (Orig. pub. 1982).

Piper, John and Wayne Grudem. 2006. *Recovering Biblical Manhood and Womanhood*. Illinois: Crossway. (Orig. pub. 1991).

Grudem, Wayne. 1999. *Bible Doctrine*. Michigan: Zondervan.

Grudem, Wayne. 1994. *Systematic Theology*. Michigan, Zondervan.

Deen, Edith. 1983. *All the Women of the Bible*. California: Harper & Row, Publishers. (Orig. pub. 1955).

Sumner, Sarah. 2003. *Men and Women in the Church*. Illinois: IVP Books.

Gardner and Associates, eds. 1994. *Who's Who in the Bible*. New York: The Reader's Digest Association.

McDonald, William. 1994. *Believer's Bible Commentary.* Tennessee: Thomas Nelson Publishers (Orig. pub. 1989).

Tenney, Merrell C. and Steven Barabas, eds. 1976. *Pictorial Bible Encyclopedia of the Bible.* 5 vols. Michigan: Zondervan. (Orig. pub 1975).

Unger, Merrell. 1985 *The New Unger's Bible Dictionary.* Illinois: The Moody Bible Institute. (Orig. pub 1957).

Vine, W.E., Merrell F. Unger, and William White, Jr. 1996. *Vine's Complete Expository Dictionary.* Tennessee: Thomas Nelson. (Orig. pub. 1984).

Alexander, Pat and David. 2009. *Handbook to the Bible.* 4th ed. Michigan: Zondervan.

Warren, Rick. 2002. *The Purpose Driven Life.* Michigan: Zondervan.

Couch, Mal, ed. 1999. *A Bible Handbook to the Acts of the Apostles*. Michigan: Kragel Publications.

Stott, John R. 1990. *The Message of Acts*. Illinois: Inter Varsity Press.

Gower, Ralph. 2005. *Manners and Customs of Bible Times*. Illinois: The Moody Bible Institute.

Random House Dictionary Database. 2001. *Webster's Universal College Dictionary.* New York: Random House, Inc. (Orig. pub. 1997).

Custis James, Carolyn. 2001. *When Life and Beliefs Collide.* Michigan: Zondervan.

Sanders. 2013. "The Father Absence Crisis in America." Assessed October 16, 2014.   www.fatherhood.org/bid/190202/The-Father-Absence-Crisis-in-America-Infograph.

U.S. Census. July 13, 2012. Accessed November 11, 2014. https://www.census.gov/population/www/socdemo/hh-fam/cps2011.html.

Nye, James. December 26, 2012. Assessed November 11, 2014.
 http://www.dailymail.co.uk/news/article-2253421.

Wikipedia. 2002. Accessed November 11, 2014.

http://en.wikipedia.org/wiki/Mandrake_ (plant)

www.ingramcontent.com/pod-product-compliance
Lightning Source LLC
Chambersburg PA
CBHW061638040426
42446CB00010B/1482